THE
IRRESISTIBLE
CON

THE IRRESISTIBLE CON

The bizarre life of a
fraudulent genius

Francis Wheen

✳ SHORT BOOKS

This paperback edition first published in 2004 by

Short Books

15 Highbury Terrace

London N5 1UP

10 9 8 7 6 5 4 3 2 1

A CIP catalogue record for this book
is available from the British Library.

ISBN 1-904095-74-7

Printed in Great Britain by
Bookmarque Ltd, Croydon, Surrey

To the memory of Bob Mellors

Prologue

'I'm very, very bad'

On 16 March 1971 the court and social page of the *Times* published its customary quota of profoundly uninteresting news. The minister of posts and telecommunications had been guest of honour at the annual dinner of the Allied Brewery Traders' Association; the parliamentary under-secretary for trade had hosted a reception for delegates to the Third International Congress on Reprography; the Bishop of Worcester had been appointed Prelate of the Order of St Michael and St George. At the foot of the page, however, was an altogether less conventional bulletin:

ADVERTISEMENT

Since scientific discoveries, unlike inventions, are not subject to patent protection and since it will take me some time before my findings are arranged suitably for publication, I wish to make the following statement:

Having investigated thoroughly and objectively all the phenomena at present haphazardly, incompletely subsumed under the blanket term 'sexual deviations' and in particular the phenomenon at present misleadingly termed 'trans-sexuality', I was able to establish the laws governing the phenomenon at present known in ethology as the 'ritualisation of displacement activities'.

My findings (a) conclusively prove that the evolution of all aspects of the behaviour of all living organisms has occurred in accordance with these laws; (b) which in turn conclusively proves that the evolution of all living organisms has occurred with identical and in essence the same laws; (c) which in turn leaves no reasonable doubt that the evolution of all inorganic matter must have occurred in an essentially homologous fashion.

These findings further (a) largely disprove Darwinian theory; (b) largely prove Lamarckian theory; (c) altogether prove beyond reasonable doubt all the main contentions of the theory at present known as 'emergent evolution'.

Bona fide scientific scrutiny is welcome.

Charlotte M. Bach (Ph.D), Highgate, N6 6PT.

As a result of this advertisement, Dr Bach was invited

by students to speak at Darwin College, Cambridge. She wrote back warning that although her theory dealt with sexual deviation they shouldn't expect anything titillating; if there was any juvenile misbehaviour she would have no hesitation in walking out. A photo was enclosed so that her hosts could recognise her at the station: 'I am tall, fair and not as young as I would like to be.'

Dr Bach was graciously received and, to her delight, seated next to a senior professor at dinner. But the lecture proved a disappointment, to her at least. When she held up a copy of *The Study of Instinct* by Niko Tinbergen – a professor at Oxford, and a leading authority on animal behaviour – she was amazed to learn that only two members of the audience had heard of him. She returned to London complaining that the evening had been a waste of time: undergraduates lacked the 'breadth of vision' to understand her ideas.

Soon afterwards the writer Colin Wilson received a 521-page typescript through the post. Since making his name in 1956 with *The Outsider* – a philosophical bestseller which was hailed by some critics as a work of precocious genius, even if others regarded it as a potpourri of mumbo-jumbo – Wilson had written more than two dozen books on sex, crime, philosophy and the occult. Surely he would see what she was getting at. In an accompanying letter, Charlotte Bach Ph.D explained that her text – '*Homo Mutans, Homo Luminens*' – was merely the 'prolegomenon' to a projected work of about 3,000 pages which would demonstrate beyond doubt that sexual deviation was the mainspring of evolution.

Wilson felt daunted by its length, its difficulty and, not least, by the fact that Dr Bach used an all-capital typewriter on orange paper. He glanced at the first 50 pages, groaned and set it aside. A few weeks later, confined to bed with flu, he tried again. 'It was hard going,' he recalled, 'but my real misgiving was that she was just an absurdly conceited female. She dismissed everyone she disagreed with – Monod, Russell, Desmond Morris – with a lofty contempt that made her sound like a combination of Madame Blavatsky, Gertrude Stein and Indira Gandhi. Yet as I persisted, this unpleasant first impression was outweighed by a sense of tremendous intelligence and an impressive grasp of European cultural history. Whether the theory was correct or not, there could be no doubt that she possessed a powerful and original mind.'

He wrote and told her so. 'I feel rather as some of the critics of my *Outsider* professed to feel – startled that anyone can have built such a huge edifice so quietly, without help. Even more astonishing, if you don't mind me saying so, because it comes from a woman, who are seldom notable for great Hegelian constructions... You are not more difficult to read than Husserl (but still not as easy as James Bond). I think it could well be Nobel Prize stuff... If you are right, then it could be as important as the theory of relativity.' In reply, Dr Bach told Wilson that she had wept for joy on reading his comments. She signed herself, 'Love, Charlotte'.

Who was Charlotte Bach? On one of his visits to London, Wilson invited her to dinner. He encountered a broad-shouldered mammoth of a woman, about six feet tall, with a deep masculine voice and a heavy Central European accent. Despite drinking plenty of wine during the meal, she seemed curiously reserved, as if she regarded most of the human race as fools. Afterwards Wilson took her back to the flat of the painter Regis de Bouvier de Cachard, where he was staying. Over several more drinks the two men at last began to learn something of her history.

Charlotte had lectured in psychology at Budapest University, where her husband was a professor; they had been driven out by the Communists in 1948. In 1965 her husband died on the operating table, and only two weeks later her son was killed in a car crash. ('At this point she burst into tears,' Wilson wrote, 'and it took a good ten minutes to soothe her.') The shock of this double bereavement had plunged her into depression and, in an attempt to fight it off, she began compiling a dictionary of psychology. While researching the section on perversions, she interviewed many people with unorthodox sexual tastes. And then came the Eureka moment: it dawned on her that perversion was the engine of human evolution. She described to Wilson and Cachard how she had leapt to her feet and shouted, 'So that's what it's all about!'

About two in the morning Charlotte departed in a taxi, paid for by Colin Wilson. 'I gave her a kiss, and she also kissed Regis. And when we got back indoors, he said: "You know, when she kissed me, she stuck her tongue halfway down my throat." We laughed about it. My own conclusion had been that Charlotte was probably lesbian, but this seemed to disprove it. It was only after her death that I realised that this was what she intended me to think.'

That December, encouraged by Wilson's interest in her theories, Dr Charlotte Bach added a postscript to her *Times* advertisement. 'Further to my announcement of 16th March 1971: My theory of emergent evolution provides adequate grounds for a flat refutation of Heisenberg's Uncertainty Principle as well as a substantial modification of Einstein's General Theory of Relativity. Bona fide scientific scrutiny is welcome.' In the spring of 1972 she began giving weekly talks at a friend's flat in Belsize Park, which she advertised in newspapers such as the *Observer* and the *New Statesman*:

Mathematical Logic and Shamanistic Ecstasies. Discussions on Human Ethology, Hampstead, Thursdays, 8pm...

Neo-Darwinism, relativity and gnosticism...

Monod, Teilhard de Chardin and alchemy...

Jung, Freud and alchemy...

Husserl, Bertrand Russell and the Book of the Dead...

About a dozen people turned up most weeks. They were expected to pay a 'voluntary contribution' of 50p, which disconcerted some visitors, since Dr Bach was so obviously an aristocrat. What need had she of 50p? Hardly anyone realised that she was probably the poorest person in the room: unable even to pay for the last *Times* announcement, she had been taken to court by the newspaper and ordered to pay off the £22 debt at a rate of two pounds per month.

Charlotte's penury, though a nuisance, did not

trouble her unduly. What preoccupied her was a craving for recognition.

Introducing herself as the leader of a new intellectual movement, she wrote to journalists and television presenters – Katherine Whitehorn, David Attenborough, the chat-show host Simon Dee – proposing that they alert the world to her discoveries. All thanked her politely but declined. Colin Wilson did his best to help by interviewing her for the London magazine *Time Out*:

> I gave her lunch at the Savage Club, then took her into a quiet corner of the lounge and asked her to explain her ideas in words of one syllable. By interjecting questions every time she seemed inclined to digress, I finally succeeded in eliciting a basic outline of her theory. But she again took the opportunity to tell me the story of the death of her husband and son, and burst into tears. It was impossible that she could have forgotten that we had been through all this before. I began to suspect that there was more than a little of the actress about Charlotte.

There was no mention of this suspicion in the article for *Time Out*, published in April 1973, which was frankly adulatory:

Charlotte Bach has developed a new theory about sex and evolution... If she is correct, or even half correct, then the implications of her theory are so tremendous that it is one of the greatest intellectual advances of the twentieth century, and she should be classified with Einstein and Freud as a revolutionary thinker.

Five years later, in his book *Mysteries*, Wilson wrote at greater length about Dr Bach's theory of evolution as inner conflict, 'all stemming from that fundamental "platonic" pull, the desire of each sex to become its opposite, or rather to blend into unity... It is this inner stress, Charlotte Bach believes, which has transformed our instincts into intellect, and which accounts for the extraordinary development of the human brain in the past half million years. The whole notion could be compared to Newton's theory of gravitation.'

First Einstein, now Newton: small wonder that, although publishers found her work 'too strange and new to have immediate appeal', her theory was nevertheless beginning to spread. 'Now she has acquired a considerable following,' Wilson wrote, 'and become something of a cult figure.'

One of the followers was A.G.E. Blake, a leading expounder of Gurdjieff's ideas, whose book *A Seminar on Time* (1980) included this handsome tribute:

> There is a marvellous phrase that I learned in London from
> Charlotte Bach, a woman of great genius who is a truly orig-
> inal thinker on time: acausal synchronicity. This phrase
> describes how the actions of beings are connected. Charlotte
> presupposes that every entity, high or low, is a focus of inten-
> tionality and reaches out into its environment to complete
> itself. What we call causality is simply the static common
> denominator of all this medley of intention; but you must
> understand that she is really talking about living time, the
> time in which things are what they are.

You must understand. Few outside Charlotte's little
group of acolytes could do so. She was too odd for
most academics to accept her; too digressive and
too damned difficult for the general public, even had
they been able to get their hands on her magnum
opus. Having persuaded herself that the letters A and
B are symbols of the male and female and that other
letters – particularly in Chinese ideogrammatic writing
– can be seen as symbolic expressions of sexual
conflict, she added a 990-page appendix to her already
sprawling typescript, headed 'Concerning the Invention
and Evolution of Writing, with special reference to

Chinese ideogrammatic writing.'

Ominously, it was marked 'Appendix 1', raising the possibility that there might be several more of the same length in due course – on shamanistic ecstasy, perhaps, or the true meaning of alchemy, or homo-sexuality among ten-spiked sticklebacks.

And so she remained a cult figure, revered by the few devotees who made regular pilgrimages to her flat in Highgate but otherwise ignored. By the spring of 1981 the once majestic figure had shrunk to a frail, weary old lady who often complained of 'having the shits' – brought on, she assumed, by food poisoning. One friend, Bob Mellors, advised her to visit a doctor, but Charlotte replied that it was years since she'd seen one and she was now 'out of the habit'.

Don Smith, a gay sadomasochist with whom she was collaborating on a book called *Sex, Sin and Evolution*, found her jaundiced and exhausted when he came to call on 10 June. 'I suppose you don't want me to ring for the ambulance and have you carted away?' he asked. 'No,' Charlotte replied firmly, before dozing off on the sofa. When Smith returned three days later, she opened the front door a couple of inches but refused to undo the security chain. 'Leave what you've brought on the step and go.'

Smith asked how she was. 'I'm very, very bad,' she replied, slamming the door.

Don Smith alerted another of the inner circle, Dr Mike Roth. When he visited the flat the next day he was forced to shout through the letter box. 'Go away,' she commanded. 'I want to die.'

On Wednesday 17 June, noticing that she hadn't taken in her milk since the weekend, one of Charlotte's neighbours called the police. A constable climbed through a window and discovered a body lying across the bed. On the bedside table was a medical dictionary open at the page dealing with cancer of the liver. A post-mortem concluded that this was indeed the cause of death, but also discovered something rather more startling. When the corpse was undressed in the mortuary, the ample breasts proved to be foam rubber, and the removal of her knickers exposed a penis. Charlotte had left instructions that in the event of her death the authorities should contact Brian Lewis, a professor at the Open University. The police duly rang to break the news about Dr Bach: 'He has died.'

Some friends were horrified to learn that their heroine had been a man in drag, and insisted that the news be suppressed. Others, such as Colin Wilson, thought it hilarious. Were the husband and child, whose memory invariably moved her to tears, mere inventions? Did she really lecture at Budapest University? What, if anything, could be believed? Had they all been taken in by a superlatively talented hoaxer?

Despite knowing Charlotte Bach for ten years, Brian Lewis never guessed her secret. Nor, apparently, did her other disciples – with the exception of Bob Mellors, a founder of the Gay Liberation Front. Back in 1973, his first thought on seeing the tall, burly, deep-voiced philosopher had been: Is this a man or a woman? He scrutinised her closely during the lecture, and Charlotte seems to have deduced what he was thinking. 'We're bound to have trouble with him,' she warned Don Smith afterwards, without specifying why. Although Mellors became an enthusiastic admirer, and swiftly abandoned his doubts about her gender, she remained wary. 'Don Smith and Charlotte had a relaxed friendship with each other, laughing and joking,' he wrote many years later. 'Charlotte never allowed that easy intimacy with me. I now realise that this must have been a deliberate policy... If she started confiding in me, there was a danger I might spot inconsistencies which would then rekindle old suspicions.'

Posthumously, however, she was happy enough for the truth to be known. In her will she bequeathed to

Mellors a collection of photographs and autobiographical essays which revealed that Charlotte Bach was in fact Baron Carl Hajdu, born in Budapest in 1920. His father had been a rich land-owning aristocrat who had lost his estates after the First World War and become a high-ranking civil servant. Carl had inherited the barony on the death of his elder brother.

But this too was fiction, and it took many years of diligent research by Bob Mellors to solve the mystery. Regrettably, he never had the chance to publish his findings: in 1996, having moved to Poland to teach English, he was murdered by an intruder in his Warsaw apartment. His worldly goods consisted of a dozen large boxes filled with notes and documents concerning Dr Bach, Baron Hajdu and other personae invented during Charlotte's lifelong search for identity. Most of this material ended up in the possession of Bob's friend Sandy Donaldson, who most generously handed it over to me. It is thanks to Bob Mellors and Sandy Donaldson that I can at last tell the story of this elusive and extraordinary character.

Chapter One

The bogus baron

Karoly Hajdu, the child who became Charlotte Bach, entered the world on 9 February 1920. His birthplace, later transformed by his fantasies into a vast baronial pile, was a small, plain, one-storey dwelling in Kispest, a working-class town near Budapest. His father, Mihaly Hajdu (pronounced hoy-doo), worked as a tailor; his mother, Roza Frits, was a coal-miner's daughter who had been orphaned at the age of six. A photograph of their wedding in 1908 shows a tall, heavily built man – characteristics inherited by Karoly – with his pretty, round-faced young bride.

Their first son, Tibor, was born in 1913. Mihaly enlisted in the army as soon as the First World War began, the following year, and was away fighting when Roza gave birth to a daughter, Vilma. Imprisoned in Italy after the Battle of the River Piave, he did not return to his family until May 1919. Roza gave birth to Karoly a mere eight months later. As an adult, Karoly Hajdu sometimes wondered about this suspiciously short pregnancy, but his mother's intensely devout Roman Catholicism should have allayed any doubts. Besides, the resemblance between father and son was unmistakable.

The similarities were not merely physical. Although Karoly was the apple of his mother's eye, in most respects he took after his father – a vain, obstinate and rather pompous man, sensitive to the smallest slight. 'Anyone who has a child will find it unrewarding to be a mother,' Karoly's sister Vilma wrote long afterwards, 'but it is not good to be a wife either. We are second fiddle. We are not allowed to deal with our own affairs. The more you look into it, the more depressing it is.'

Roza took out her frustration on her husband, whom she berated incessantly for his apparent lack of ambition. Perhaps in the hope of pleasing her, he moved the family to Budapest in 1923, renting a small tailoring shop on Raday Street. They were still poor, all living in one little room upstairs. Mihaly's customers, by contrast, included many rich and cultured gentlemen, whose amplitude of knowledge and experience made a profound impression on the young Karoly. His dream of reinventing himself had already begun.

He taught himself to read and write at the age of four by pointing to letters in the newspaper and asking his parents what they were. Decades later, Charlotte Bach would boast that as a child she had been intensely curious about things that most people took for granted; this, she suggested, was probably how she came to devise a revolutionary new theory of evolution. To illustrate the point, she recalled that as a four-year-old she had once walked to the local telephone box, picked up the receiver and talked to the operator: having never used a phone before, she wanted to say hello and hear someone reply.

Karoly started his elementary education in 1926 and progressed four years later to the Andras Fay Gimnazium, the Hungarian equivalent of a grammar school. Since secondary education was neither compulsory nor free (though fees were modest), it implies some effort on a poor tailor's part for all three of his children to have attended such a school.

A book about hypnosis written by one of Karoly Hajdu's later incarnations, 'Michael Karoly', includes a case history of a transvestite which is almost certainly autobiographical:

At school he was a mediocre scholar. He always wanted to run away and leave everything behind. He would work out in his imagination a very clever theft and decide that he would go into hiding with the proceeds until the search for him ended and then escape to some distant country.

One day it struck him that the best way to disguise himself would be as a girl. From then on all his fantasies of flight involved changing into women's clothes. At school there were several homosexual friendships between boys themselves or with older men from outside, but he was never approached by anyone. He never took part in the communal sessions of masturbation in which most of his schoolmates indulged.

Formal academic work held little appeal for this daydreaming loner. 'I loved putting my teachers through the hoops,' he wrote. 'They in turn loved proving at exam time that I wasn't so bloody clever.' Outside the classroom, however, he was an insatiable autodidact. 'When I was 11 years old, I read a six-volume history of the world – 2,300 pages. At 12, I read Freud's *Introduction to Psychoanalysis* and *The Interpretation of Dreams*. At 15, I read Kant's *Critique of Pure Reason*. Mind you, I'm not pretending that I understood most of it; it's just that the *Boy's Own* type of reading did not appeal to me. I gave up reading novels at the age of ten.'

Since he was also an accomplished liar, one might suspect him of exaggeration here. But the general truth of his account has been confirmed by Vilma, who says that her brother spent most of his spare time alone in the public library, immersed in philosophy and mathematics: 'Many times we had to go and fetch him, otherwise he wouldn't have come home.' With such precocious interests, it is no surprise that Karoly had few friends of his own age: he was regarded as a very odd boy indeed. In the middle of a conversation, his mother recalled, he would suddenly start talking about something completely different, and then rejoin the conversation some minutes later as if he had just returned from a different world. His explanation was that he was arguing with himself.

In 1931 the Hajdus moved to an apartment block at 9 Felsoerdosor, in a slightly smarter part of the city, and for the next three years Karoly attended the Zsigmond Kemeny Technical High School in nearby Szondi Street. He paid little attention to his studies: puberty had struck. 'I began masturbating at the age of ten,' he wrote, 'and haven't stopped since.' According to his sister, he ran away from home once when he was 11 and again when he was 13 – this time getting as far as Austria and staying away for three weeks. In later years Roza Hajdu reminded her son of the grief and anxiety he had provoked:

> When you were young you caused me many sleepless nights. I don't suppose you remember that when you were 13 I went to search for you night after night in the park. I know that you have always been a good boy, but you always tried to escape from something and you would never say what that something was. You always lived a life of fantasy and never found anyone to understand you.

The 'something' may well have been Karoly's budding awareness of his own feminine characteristics. Charlotte Bach admitted as much when she wrote that the pubertal boy with an emerging mother complex 'often tries to deny his archetypal mother image by trying to run away from home, that is, by trying to sever the apron strings of the flesh-and-blood mother'.

In these years of early adolescence a normal lad would probably be exploring his masculinity in the company of other boys. But Karoly tagged along with his sister and her friends, hypnotised by the feminine mystique and determined to understand it. In one of the glossy magazines which she read avidly, Vilma noticed a picture of a dance act with two female impersonators. 'Poor unfortunate things!' she exclaimed. Karoly did not think them unfortunate at all: 'They looked so lovely and beautiful.'

There was one influential male presence in Karoly's life at this time. In a letter to Colin Wilson, Charlotte Bach revealed how she had first heard of the Christian heretic Giordano Bruno through a man named Monsieur Jacques Sturm:

I must have been 11 or 12 years old. M. Sturm was explaining to my sister – who, as you recall, is six years older than I am – about Spinoza's system and I happened to be around without either listening or grasping anything much... So M. Jacques Sturm, the crazy genius, must have already known and understood about Bruno all that present-day scholars are beginning to discover, and that philosophers 50 or more years ago, when M. Sturm must have been first getting acquainted with the subject, did not know or chose not to know. I am always astonished about the number of bits and pieces that went into my work which I can trace back to my earliest teens and to M. Sturm.

In a curriculum vitae compiled in 1971, Charlotte described M. Sturm as 'an extraordinarily intelligent (bordering on the genius, but rather dissolute) house tutor', who had introduced her to the works of Jung, Plato, Kant, Kierkegaard, Nietzsche, Adam Smith, Malthus and Marx – and all by the time she was 15 or so. Elsewhere, she added that this 'house tutor' was also hopelessly irresponsible: 'He would write a three-page poem – and a good one at that – about a girl in love, while chatteringly explaining the binomial theorem. Then he would disappear for three days because he'd got embroiled in a game of cards in a shady club.'

By the time she wrote these reminiscences, Charlotte was pretending to be an aristocrat. Of course she had no house tutor. Nevertheless, Sturm wasn't one of her inventions; Vilma remembered him too. He first turned up on the door-step 'selling something or other'. Since the family was playing cards, he then offered to show them a few card tricks instead. Thereafter he was a regular evening visitor, regaling the Hajdus with tales of his exploits: when not writing short stories for newspapers and screenplays for films, he said, he appeared in a circus performing feats of mental arithmetic. One of Mihaly's customers was so impressed by this that he arranged for a competition with an adding machine.

Sturm proved to be the faster calculator.

Despite his shabbiness and raffish habits, Sturm became a favourite household pet. After the Second World War the family made efforts to trace him, not least because he was Karoly's 'only real friend'; but without success. It seems likely that he met the same end as so many other Jews in Hungary.

• • •

'Up to about 14, my best friend was my sister,' Karoly Hajdu said. 'After that, my brother.' Tibor Hajdu, seven years older than Karoly, was by then working as a clerk in a newspaper office. In the evenings he played the trumpet in a band.

There were certainly discernible changes to Karoly's life and character in this period. Joe Marfy, a school-mate, says that he became a scheming and rather unpleasant youth who would borrow things without returning them and stole any money he saw lying around. At the age of 15 he was transferred to the Bolyai Technical High School – perhaps, Marfy surmised, because the previous school disliked his attitude. (According to Karoly, 'one of the masters told my father I had a superiority complex'.) It was also at 15 that he lost his virginity to a prostitute. His most resonant and abiding memory of this otherwise unsatisfactory encounter was the sight of the woman putting on her silk stockings afterwards as she dressed for her job as a barmaid.

In one of her manuscripts, Charlotte Bach reflected on the interior life of the cross-dresser. 'Most transvestites mention, mostly with some pride, fairly long periods in their childhood, usually between the ages of six and 11, when they behaved as ordinary boys with no more than a minor predilection for girls' games and dressing up, though, unlike most boys, they always enjoyed girls' company. Then, usually about the age of ten or 12, they come face to face with the larger realities of the external world.' The boy has disappointed his parents, and is resigned to his inadequacy. Ambition wilts. He senses that if he were a girl he would be loved more. 'Then he comes across something soft and silky. This is something that has never left him. From early childhood, when his mother was in a not-so-close mood, he found solace in a soft silky pillow or something soft and silky that belonged to his mother.'

How to reconcile this yearning for the sensual comforts of infancy with the sexual allure of a prostitute's stockings? Karoly tried to suppress his awakening desires, knowing that banishment from Eden was the penalty for eating the fruit of that forbidden tree. He sought refuge in the company of pre-adolescents such as Eva Neuenstein, daughter of a baroness, who met him at a skating club ball when she was 12 and he 17. Eva, wearing white socks and a short white skating dress, was astonished when this 'grown-up' (as he seemed to her) asked for a dance. She can still remember what she dreamed that night: when she was 18, this gallant suitor would come back and marry her. A few days later, however, misgivings began to set in. Wasn't it slightly strange that a young man should choose to dance with a mere child? Why did he seem so afraid of adult women?

Karoly Hajdu's life at this period can be seen as a struggle against maturity in all its manifestations. His older siblings, Tibor and Vilma, left home as soon as they were old enough and shared a flat together; Karoly remained with his parents. By dropping out of school he avoided the traditional post-graduation ritual of drinking all afternoon and then visiting a brothel. Nor was he in any hurry to find a job: apart from a six-day stint as a clerk in the Hungarian Film Office, he seems to have been unemployed for several years. When his call-up papers arrived, after Hungary declared war on Russia in June 1941, Karoly somehow managed to obtain a 'student exemption' for a year. Yet he was not entirely idle. At an early age, from observing customers in his father's shop, Karoly had realised that there were plenty of wealthy people who could be parted from their money. The trick was to meet them. In October 1942 he forged a birth certificate on which he renamed himself Karoly Mihaly Balazs Agoston Hajdu, son of the Baron of Szadelo and Balkany. He had cards printed with the baronial title, and acquired a cigarette case embellished with a coat of arms and the letters 'SB'. But before he could put these conman's props into service he was drafted into the 4th battalion of the Railway Builders' Regiment stationed at St Endre, about ten miles north of Budapest. Weeks later he wangled himself a transfer to the army propaganda unit – where, he told Joe Marfy, he stole two cameras and sold them on the black market.

After the Italian surrender of September 1943, Hungary attemped to convey, through secret diplomacy, her readiness to yield to the Western allies. Hitler decided he needed a more steadfast supporter on his eastern flank, and offered Hungary a choice between outright German occupation or a Nazi-approved government. The Hungarians duly installed a collaborationist regime, but suffered what amounted to an occupation anyway. German soldiers became a common sight in

Budapest; Jews were rounded up and sent to the death camps. In later life Karoly claimed to have served in the German SS, and would prove it by displaying a photograph of himself in SS uniform, complete with an Iron Cross. It was a perverse thing to boast about, especially since he was in fact in the Hungarian army. But the photo confirms that even as a young man he enjoyed dressing up and creating alternative identities for himself.

In October 1944, with the advancing Russian army now within striking distance of Budapest, Hitler appointed the head of the Hungarian Nazi Party, Ferenc Szalasi, as National Leader. Life in the capital deteriorated sharply. Armed gangs roamed the streets demanding jewellery and cash.

'As winter set in,' the Hungarian historian Paul Ignotus writes, 'with ice floes blocking the Danube, and the people of Budapest shivering in cellars beneath the thunder of Soviet gunfire and Allied air raids, the Hungarian Nazis took their final toll in blood and property, no longer bothering themselves about deportation when railway wagons were not available, but shooting their victims on the spot and shovelling them into the river... By the end of the war some two thirds of Hungary's Jewish popula-tion, including 40 per cent of those in Budapest, were exterminated.'

Some of Karoly's relations suspect that he may have been looting abandoned houses. He certainly seemed remarkably prosperous when Eva Neuenstein met him in the Hungaria-Ritz hotel. He told her that he was 'helping Jews'. Knowing that desperate Jewish families in Budapest would offer everything they had in return for sanctuary or escape, she wondered if her old dancing partner had profited from their predicament.

A clue to Karoly's behaviour at the time can be found in a novel he would write some years later, *Siobhan*, where the narrator delivers a bizarre post-coital monologue to the lady of the title:

What is the most dreadful thing anyone can do? To kill another human being in cold blood for no reason? Well, I have done that. I'm not talking about killing in action. One doesn't think about that. Not a normal person. Why did I do it? I have pondered this question for 20 years, but I have not found the answer.

Of course, to understand it really you ought to have been there. It was 1944, just a day or two before Christmas. Budapest was completely surrounded by the Russian army. The town was under constant bombardment. No electricity, no telephones, no public transport, no nothing. There was a full curfew from 8pm. The Hungarian army was already in an advanced state of disintegration. I was an officer [sic], my papers were in order, but even I wasn't supposed to be out at night, except on duty. As it happened I had been boozing with some chaps and I started walking home, well stoked up, after midnight.

When I was only a few corners away from home, I was stopped by a youngster and asked to identify myself. He couldn't have been more than 15. With a tommy gun and a brace of hand grenades. Because the army was already falling to pieces, the Hungarian Nazi Party armed these children for guard duty. None of them had a clue about politics; they just enjoyed strutting around with real guns. What child wouldn't? I was tired, sleepy and drunk and just wanted to get home to bed. So I told him to buzz off. He levelled the gun at me and demanded that I go with him to the Nazi Party headquarters, which was not very far, but in the opposite direction to where I lived.

Now listen carefully, because this part is important. I knew that my papers were OK. I would have been released within half an hour, in all probability. But I couldn't be sure. You see, it was not the army but the Nazi headquarters he was taking me to. On the other hand, I'm sure I could have insisted on my unit commander being contacted. You see, the Nazis had respect for rank. As against that, I really had no right to be on the streets after curfew. Then again, I could have changed my tune to the boy and I am fairly certain he would have let me go, because he didn't know chalk from cheese.

You know what I did? As we were walking along side by side, I fell back a step, pulled my gun from its holster – that shows what a stupid kid he was, he didn't even disarm me – and shot him in the back of the head. And just walked away. In those days, a shot after dark didn't disturb anyone.

Since then I have often wondered why I did it. It wasn't really necessary... The only conclusion I could come to was that I was tired and bored and I couldn't be bothered. So a young life came to an end. Now you know what I mean when I ask the unanswerable question: why does a man do what he does?

Siobhan was written in the 1960s. However, Karoly told the same story to Bela Tamasi, a Hungarian whom he met in London in 1950. Tamasi, appalled, felt sure that it was true. Karoly added that he had confessed the sin to a priest shortly before leaving Hungary in 1948, but did not receive absolution.

One possible motive for his savage treatment of the boy is that his papers were not in order after all: like many young soldiers, Karoly deserted from his unit shortly before the city fell rather than leave with the German army. He spent three weeks holed up in the cellar with his parents while Soviet troops stormed into Pest. When the worst of the fighting was over, he emerged to find a devastated landscape of rubble and corpses, with odd arms and legs sticking up out of the snow like jettisoned firewood.

Charlotte Bach later spoke of going to cocktail parties 'as usual' after the siege: everything swiftly returned to normal, she said, except that the guests were Russians instead of Germans. The 25-year-old Karoly decided to complete his secondary education privately, matriculating in 1946. His grades, though poor, were just good enough for him to enrol in the economics department of the Technical University in Budapest. His record book includes a photograph of the new undergraduate in a dinner jacket, white tie and winged collar, the very model of a young aristocrat. It was also at about this time that he began wearing a monocle, purely as an affectation.

Academically, his university career was thoroughly undistinguished; after the end of the first half-year semester he seems to have given up attending classes altogether. But vanity would eventually transform this dismal record into something more fitting for a great intellectual. 'Frankly, I think my theory and its likely effects are infinitely more monstrous than Teller's H-Bomb,' Charlotte Bach wrote to David Attenborough at the BBC 30 years later. 'Funny that he was at one time (before my time) a lecturer at the same university where I held a lectureship. Perhaps there is, after all, some irritable old boy up there watching us.'

Charlotte Bach also claimed to have been imprisoned by the Communists – and for once he was telling the truth. Karoly's sister Vilma says that he was held for a few months at the Central Remand Prison in Budapest, although she never knew why: theft or black-marketeering, most likely. Soon after emigrating to England, three years later, he sent the local newspaper in Essex a gruesome account of jail life:

One night a young man who was in the same cell with me returned from questioning with broken ribs, no teeth and a terribly shattered face. He could hardly move, yet half an hour later he was taken back and soon we heard a scream and he was just before our window lying on the courtyard and we were told that he 'committed suicide' by jumping out of a third-floor window. I could quote hundreds of other cases, many of them much more dreadful than those above-mentioned. The Nazi police state and Gestapo was only an unpromising apprentice compared to the Communist master. You can take my word for it. I have seen both.

Vilma, who had been employed during the war by the electrical manufacturer AEG, left Hungary to start a new life in Venezuela when she heard that the Communists were rounding up anyone who had worked for German firms. Karoly decided that he too must escape. Having no passport or visa, he contacted an old army colleague, Paul Peters, who was helping to smuggle refugees out.

On 11 January 1948, after saying a tearful farewell to his parents, Karoly boarded a train for Austria with Peters. They got off two stops before the frontier, hid until nightfall and then began a perilous yomp through the frozen fields and woods – two miles to the border, followed by 15 miles of the Russian-occupied buffer zone – before reaching the sanctuary of the British sector. From surviving official documents we know that by 11 February he was lodged with a Frau Wittmann in Graz, sharing a room with four other refugees. He registered as 'Karl Hajdu, university student'. Karoly's first reinvention of himself had begun: one of Frau Wittmann's daughters remembers him as a courteous but rather formal man who insisted on being addressed as Baron Hajdu – though his German was so bad that it was difficult to understand him.

Karoly did speak excellent, self-taught English, however, and it was England on which he now set his sights. After the war, because of a labour shortage, the British government had decided to admit refugees who were willing to spend their first three years in restricted occupations such as mining and brick-making. Given the overwhelming scale of the refugee problem, selection was none too rigorous and anyone with obvious talents – such as speaking the language – would be accepted quickly. On 22 April 1948, after a long train journey across Europe, he boarded a boat to Harwich.

• • •

His first disappointment, as England came into view, was that it was the flat Essex coast rather than the white cliffs of Dover. But Britain had plentiful opportunities, and he felt well equipped to seize them. He was tall, good-looking and smartly dressed. Unlike most of his fellow-passengers, he spoke English. Britain still had an aristocracy: perhaps he could find a niche there. In the course of the journey he had anglicised his name to Carl and started working up the fiction that he had been a university lecturer. Perhaps he would establish himself as a man of letters instead.

From Harwich the refugees went to a reception camp at West Wratting in Cambridgeshire, a former RAF camp where they were housed in Nissen huts. Carl held himself aloof, even from other Hungarians. Regarding him as a snooty fantasist, they happily reciprocated. But he did not stay long. Saved from the indignity of a factory or a mine by his fluency in the language, he was signed up as an interpreter and returned to Harwich.

Carl and a Pole named Konrad Rozycki installed themselves in an office at the labour exchange. Their job was to assist the new arrivals when the boats came in twice a week. In practice, however, they had little to do, since incoming refugees were met by British officials and put on a train forthwith. His main function was to provide unwitting entertainment to other workers at the labour exchange, who thought him deliciously absurd: he would arrive every morning with his hat and umbrella, a coat draped elegantly around his shoulders and a copy of the *Daily Telegraph* under his arm. His days were spent reading the newspaper and books from the public library. He looked older than his 28 years. No one believed he was a baron, but Carl was too conceited to suspect that anyone might rumble him. On a trip to London one weekend, after visiting the Hungarian Club, he presented himself at the house of Captain Montague Orczy-Barstow, son of the Baroness Orczy who had written *The Scarlet Pimpernel*, and pretended to be a lost scion of the Orczy family. Captain Barstow made inquiries among émigré Hungarians and received uniformly bad reports. Nevertheless, the bogus baron continued to turn up at the front door from time to time until eventually Barstow ordered him to go away. Never one to take a rebuttal lightly, Carl bombarded Captain Barstow and anyone who knew him with abusive letters for weeks.

Carl's friend from Budapest, Joe Marfy, reached England a few months after him and was despatched to the Staveley iron and steelworks in Yorkshire. One cold winter's morning the foreman told Marfy that an important person wished to see him in the general manager's office. It was Hajdu, impeccably attired in a tweed coat and velour hat. He winked, and murmured in Hungarian: 'Call me baron.' Marfy, though surprised, duly greeted the visitor: 'Ah, Baron Hajdu!' Once they had been left alone, Carl explained that a title would enable him to succeed, adding that it had already given him an entrée to 'good social circles'. When he asked if Marfy required anything, his friend answered jokingly

'Give us a pound!'. A pound was three days' food; but, to his astonishment, Carl opened a bulging wallet and handed one over. Clearly, the baron had found ways of supplementing his meagre income. He and a colleague from Harwich, a Mr Hawkins, were suspected by customs officers of running 'some kind of fiddle' at the port. Hawkins fled when he discovered he was under observation; Carl, unassailably self-confident, brazened it out. Workers at the labour exchange noticed that he always seemed to have more clothing coupons than anyone else, and had even managed to acquire orange-juice coupons which were meant only for children.

Although he was gradually mutating into an English gent, Baron Hajdu would make the most of his Hungarian background when there was some advantage to be gained. The decision by the new Communist regime to put Cardinal Minszenty on trial – which provoked outrage in Britain – provided just such an opportunity. The *Harwich & Dovercourt Standard* of 18 February 1949 reported a local protest meeting: 'A Hungarian nobleman, a refugee now living at Harwich where he is in employment, spoke of personal experience of the menace of Communism at a meeting at Frinton, on Friday.' A week later, the paper interviewed this noble character:

No man living in Harwich today can lay claim to greater understanding of events behind the 'iron curtain' than 29-year-old Baron Balkanyi, interpreter to the Ministry of Labour, who lives in Station Road, Harwich. His name, other than the province of which he was baron, he cannot reveal for publication because his parents are still living in Hungary.

The following month, the 'Baron Balkanyi' ventured on to the correspondence page. 'I have,' he wrote, 'always followed with interest your "Letters to the Editor" column. Up to now I did not consider myself entitled to interfere with local arguments, but since lately a few times the Hungarian People's Court has been mentioned, I feel obliged to add a few words to the debate.' He described the brutal treatment meted out to dissidents, and argued that a similar Communist takeover could happen in England with surprising ease.

A local Communist, Mrs Cook, refused to believe his horror stories. 'What evidence has anyone of labour camps, etc., except the "evidence" of such fevered imaginations as "Balkanyi's"?' she demanded. Balkanyi replied a week later: 'I have had many good arguments with Communists, but this was the first in which my personal experiences were called "feverish imagination".

44

No doubt, I have tried to avoid any arguments with women.' Mrs Cook rose to the bait. 'He need not be afraid of arguing with a woman,' she riposted. 'I believe (unlike the Nazis) in equality for the sexes.'

Carl was genuinely appalled by what had happened in Hungary, and yet he couldn't help being impressed by the Communists' ruthless efficiency. There seemed to be something irresistible about their rise to power, as if history was on their side. He worked these thoughts into a novel, which transposed events from Communist Hungary to a hypothetical Britain of the future. The book was unpublished, and indeed almost unreadably turgid. More surprisingly, he wrote a short essay – 'The I-Centred Universe' – on the psychology of perception, which argued that only at brief moments, in love, can we ever truly share our world with another. It prefigures many of Charlotte Bach's ideas; after abandoning the piece, however, Hajdu kept this side of his intellect hidden for many years. Instead, he tried his hand at lighter fiction, including 'The Fable of the Monocle' (a short story about an exiled aristocrat) and 'Good Business' (an amusing yarn about a confidence trickster). The choice of subjects speaks for itself. Following the death of his father in December 1949, and his mother's subsequent emigration to join Vilma in

Venezuela, Carl was on his own. He could be whoever he wanted to be. A conman? An aristocrat? Or both?

The flood of refugees into Britain ceased in April 1950, and with it Carl's duties. His conditions of entry still restricted the work he was allowed to do; of the options available, he thought the hotel trade most suitable. He found a job as receptionist and bookkeeper at the Valley of the Rocks hotel in Lynton, North Devon – at the very opposite end of the country from Harwich.

He stayed there for only a few months before heading for London, and no record survives of his brief career in the West Country apart from three photographs. One shows Carl and a woman on the seafront. In the second, he is with a different woman in Clovelly, along the coast from Lynton. The third, with Carl and yet another woman on a train, is inscribed: 'You and I, 18 July 1950.'

Her identity is unknown, but in a later picture she and Carl are stepping out in the West End of London, near Leicester Square. It was probably taken that autumn, by which time he had found temporary work as a general assistant at the British Council in London. Those who met him in this period noticed that Carl seemed to prefer the company of rich, older women. But what were his sexual impulses? In an unpublished article, he refers to a war widow with 'fabulous legs' whom he met in Harwich:

At the time nylons were still scarce and I managed to buy her half a dozen pairs. On the day I was supposed to give her the present she called the date off… I went to bed early and started reading. Some time later, I just put the book down, went to get a pair of those nylon stockings, put them on, admired my legs for a few minutes, then masturbated with a hitherto unexperienced intensity.

The moment I ejaculated I was filled with shame and despised myself beyond description. I tore the stockings off in shreds and vowed never to do it again.

Two years later, at the end of 1950, his transvestite feelings surfaced again – prompted, it seems, by depression or even desperation. He was living in a boarding-house in Earl's Court, but after finishing at the British Council he had no job and no prospect of one. One day a friend left a suitcase of his wife's dresses and underwear with Hajdu for safe keeping. Carl tried them all on. The next morning, disgusted with himself, he asked the friend to remove the case.

A few months later [he recalled] my situation was getting

worse and I found myself gradually buying and building up a secret – in a way, secret even from myself – collection of female garments. I didn't dress often, perhaps not more than once a month, even less; but the wardrobe grew steadily.

Then came a purge all transvestites are familiar with. I decided that all this was just a lot of nonsense and wanted to get rid of the lot. But how? Throwing them in the dustbin would have been impractical. Questions might be asked. I didn't have the heart to burn them as they were good stuff. Giving them away would have provoked awkward questions and improbable answers. So I used to pack them up in small parcels and 'lose' them on buses, park benches and on the street. But hardly had I got rid of them than I started buying more.

By now Carl had been in the country for three years and was no longer restricted in the type of employment he could take. As a natural aristocrat, he would have preferred not to work at all, of course, but meanwhile he was obliged to return to the only trade he knew. In May 1951 he started as a receptionist at the Plough and Harrow Hotel in Birmingham. He lasted six weeks. Next stop was Brighton, and six months at the Hotel Metropole.

His spell on the south coast had two important

consequences. While he was there, the British Parliament began discussing a Bill to ban stage hypnotism as a public entertainment, provoked by a notorious performance in 1948 at the Brighton Hippodrome, where a woman had been hypnotised to cry like a baby. Extensive coverage of the debate aroused Carl's interest in hypnosis – which, as we shall see, would eventually become yet another of his many obsessions. It was also in Brighton that he met his future wife, Phyllis, a divorcee who dreamed of becoming an actress. There are two accounts of their courtship. In his version, they met in a hotel lobby and were in bed within half an hour. According to Phyllis, however, Carl wooed her most romantically, sending single roses, tiny boxes of handmade chocolates and a pair of kid button gloves. Either story would be true to his character.

At the end of 1951 Carl Hajdu returned to London and found a vacancy for a barman at the Pigalle, a famous night-spot in Piccadilly, where he became known as 'Mr Carl'. Phyllis followed dutifully, installing herself in a flat in North Finchley and working as a bookkeeper at a firm of builders in the West End. Her seven-year-old son Peter, who had been staying with an aunt, moved back with his mother. But Carl himself was only an occasional weekend visitor – not least because he was 'profoundly in love' with someone else, a married businesswoman from Sussex who often came to stay at his two-room apartment in London. 'She too was older than I, but warm, soft and beautiful,' he wrote in his fictionalised autobiography. 'I wanted very much to marry her, but it was not practical. I saw that she couldn't live without her children. So she went back to her husband... Then one day I got a job in the West Indies.'

This last sentence, surprisingly enough, is true. At the Pigalle one night Carl met Benson Greenall, an international entrepreneur who hoped to turn the then undeveloped Cayman Islands into a winter resort for rich Americans. The Baron Hajdu appeared to be just the sort of classy, sophisticated cosmopolitan who would impress the customers, and soon talked himself into a job. In November 1952 the London *Evening Standard* ran a gossip paragraph about Greenall and his wife, described as the 'king and queen' of the Caymans. 'Next month they are going out from London,' it reported, 'to pursue plans to develop hotels and farms there. An airstrip will be finished in December. Baron Carl Hajdu, a Hungarian nobleman, who was once a Budapest university professor, is going with them to be director of the beach club Greenall has built.' This was the first that his bosses at the Pigalle had heard of Mr Carl's intentions. They sacked him at once.

When he arrived in Jamaica, after six weeks of unemployment, he didn't even have the ten-shilling landing fee. On Grand Cayman he was impressed by the silver sand and warm sea, and by the luxury of the hotel. But a month later he was at Nassau in the Bahamas, writing to inform his fiancée that the great adventure was over. 'By the time you receive this letter I shall be in London, probably with you. Of course, when I get back I shall tell you all about it, so there is no point in writing it now. Believe me, I am looking forward very much to seeing you again and I have been thinking of you all the time I was away.'

What went wrong? A friend of Benson Greenall's wife, Melisande, remembers Baron Carl Hajdu's Cayman interlude well. 'He was only here just a few days over a month. Mel said to me she could not stand him. If Mel and I went out of the hotel he would always welcome us back in by bowing and kissing our hands and drinking all the Greenalls' Tia Maria. Mel repeatedly said he must go.' Carl thought about joining his mother and sister in Venezuela, but the travel arrangements were too complicated. And so Phyllis got her man.

Chapter Two

'My honour is at stake'

Carl Hajdu returned to London on 27 January 1953. Eight days later he married Phyllis Mary Rodgers at Hendon Register Office. On the wedding certificate she named her grandfather as her father and described him as the director of a shipbuilding firm; in fact, he had been an electrical fitter. Not to be outdone, Carl elevated his own father to the 'Ministry of Industry'. The newly-weds were perfectly matched when it came to self-aggrandising fantasy. But Phyllis was happy to believe that she had really become a baroness. Almost the only correct details on the form are the dates of birth. The groom was 32, his bride 29.

Phyllis's family lived in the small working-class town of Pembroke Dock, South Wales. At the time of her birth, in 1923, her mother had been unmarried, so she had been taken in by grandparents who had brought her up as their own child. As a free-spirited, vivacious girl she chafed at their strict rectitude, and left home as soon as she could – at the age of 18 – to marry for the first time. By 1948 she was a divorcee with a three-year-old son. It was then that she had handed Peter to an aunt and decamped to Brighton.

Short and plump, certainly no great beauty, Phyllis nevertheless dressed with theatrical panache: she told a friend how important it was to ensure that every head turned when you entered a room. As a connoisseur of women's clothing, Carl admired her style. 'When I married her, I was sure all my transvestism was over,' he recalled, 'yet for some inexplicable reason I didn't throw my things away, but put them into storage. For five years I paid half-a-crown a week for the contents of a couple of suitcases which I had no intention of using.' Her brisk efficiency appealed to him, too. When Carl wondered what to do next after the Cayman débâcle, it was she who came up with the idea of starting an accommodation agency. Three months after the wedding, from a small office over a restaurant in Paddington, the K Bureau opened for business. Carl and Phyllis moved into a furnished flat nearby, in Bouverie Place.

Adverts for the Bureau in the local paper offered rooms where 'children and coloured people' were welcome. Had Carl been offering a fair deal, this inclusiveness would have been exemplary. But honesty was never his policy: the willingness to accept allcomers proved only that he was trawling the lower end of the market. This was the era of vicious and exploitative Rachmanesque landlords, and Carl was happy to capitalise on the plight of the homeless. From the outset, he openly flouted the 1953 Accommodation Agencies Act, which had made it illegal to charge prospective tenants for a list of addresses. In March 1954 he was taken to court for imposing a fee of two guineas for just such a service. Pleading ignorance, he got off with an absolute discharge, but four months later he was back in court for the same offence. This time he was fined ten guineas plus costs. Unable to continue with the K Bureau, he reconstituted his agency as the Apartment Lessors' Association and moved to a two-room office at 56 Edgware Road, near Marble Arch. The principle of the new venture was that landlords would pay a subscription, in return for which he would find tenants, manage properties and collect rents. Towards the end of 1954 Phyllis left her job at the building firm to work full-time for the Association; a trainee osteopath, Cynthia

Holmes-Brand, was hired as a telephonist.

After the last run-in with the law they had to be careful not to charge flat-seekers, but there was a collecting box on the front desk for customers who wished to make a 'voluntary' donation. Since the landlords, who were supposed to be financing the enterprise, also seemed to regard their subscriptions as optional, the Association teetered constantly on the edge of ruin.

That December Carl was up in court yet again, for failing to register his business name. He insisted that the Apartment Lessors' Association was not a business at all but a non-profit friendly society (though he hadn't registered it as that either). The magistrates fined him £15 with ten guineas' costs.

The baron erupted in fury at the unfairness of it all. Here he was, a noble fellow who had fled the oppressive regime in Hungary and tried to establish himself as a responsible, hard-working British citizen – only to suffer persecution from another hard-faced gang of police and bureaucrats. His flamboyant indignation was reported in the *Daily Mail* of 5 February 1955:

The Hungarian consulate in London last night refused to detain 35-year-old Baron Carl Hajdu, who was sentenced to six years' imprisonment in 1948 by the Hungarian People's

Government. He gave himself up at the consulate headquarters in Eaton Square at 8pm.

Ten minutes later he walked out, a free man. At the doorway he was interviewed by a young Communist official holding a ping-pong bat and ball. They spoke heatedly in Hungarian. Another Communist official listened.

Then one told me: 'We cannot detain this man now. First we must contact Budapest, so I suggest that Baron Hajdu report to us between 11am and 1pm tomorrow.' The consulate door was locked again.

The baron had driven to the consulate after losing an appeal against a £25 fine imposed at Marylebone Court for failing to register the Apartment Lessors' Association as a company... Standing in the rain outside the consulate, he said: 'My honour is at stake – the court destroyed it.'

Now he preferred to return to Hungary 'to face a charge of which I am guilty' rather than remain in London, with his wife and ten-year-old son.

'I was a lecturer at Budapest University,' he said. 'I escaped to Britain while awaiting trial on a charge of activities against the People's Government.' He looked at the locked door. 'But this,' he said, 'is final... Now I don't think I want to go back home.'

It was all too typical of Hajdu that, when in a corner,

he adamantly refused to admit that he was wrong but hit out in such a way as to exacerbate his plight. The incident seems to have alerted Duncan Webb, legendary crime reporter of the *Sunday People*, who turned up incognito at the Apartment Lessors' Association soon afterwards posing as a flat-seeker. Like any other customer, he was invited to put five shillings in the collection box. The consequence was a lengthy article exposing Carl's ingenious 'little dodges for getting round the law'.

His family in Venezuela hadn't heard from him for a year. The long silence made his 69-year-old mother anxious, but Vilma had sagely advised her: 'Karoly only writes when he is in trouble, so don't worry – he must be doing all right.' Sure enough, he now resumed the correspondence. His mother already knew about the histrionic performance at the consulate: she informed him that his 'bad reputation' had even reached Hungary. Nevertheless, she enclosed some money. One of Phyllis's Welsh uncles also helped out with a bank loan of £250; needless to add, he never saw it again.

Could destitution be far behind? Not at all. In October 1955, to the amazement of their few friends, Carl and Phyllis moved into a luxury flat in Cadogan Gardens, Chelsea, with a white grand piano in the first-floor living-room. Visitors goggled at the opulence. But this apparent change in fortune depended on sleight of hand. The house was owned by a retired opera singer and, in return for managing the property, Carl had been given the flat at a reduced rate, which he never paid anyway. Meanwhile, he earned money by hiring out the main room for meetings and drama rehearsals. He also sub-let his old flat in Paddington at twice the official rent, pocketed the difference – and, in a grand gesture of baronial insouciance, even left behind an unpaid gas bill for the new tenant to settle.

Early in 1956 Carl was again charged with failing to register his business name. This time he admitted the offence, while adding in mitigation that he derived no income from the association and lived on occasional subventions from his poor mother in South America. Unmoved by this sob-story, the magistrates imposed a fine of £30 with ten guineas costs. They were undoubtedly justified in disbelieving his plea of poverty. Among Charlotte Bach's effects is a 1956 member's card for Carl Hajdu at the Maisonette, a fashionable and expensive drinking club in Mayfair. (Ruby Lloyd, the owner, recalls with pride one summer's night when she had 11 maharajahs on the roof.) Nor could the widow's mite have covered the cost of hospitality at Cadogan Gardens: now that the baron at last had a place befitting his status he enjoyed playing the extravagant host, cultivating the acquaintance of authors and aristocrats.

One of many guests was the popular Hungarian author George Mikes, who had recently published a humorous book about Italians. On 15 October the William Hickey column in the *Daily Express* reported:

> Signor Vincenzo Caputo, of Pisa, who has challenged London humorist author George Mikes to a duel for 'offending the honour and dignity of Italians' in a new book, has not had long to wait for offers of a second. Baron Carl Hajdu, formerly assistant lecturer at the Budapest University of Economics, who now lives in London, tells me he would like to act for the signor, and adds: 'I admire Mr Mikes for accepting the challenge as a true Hungarian gentleman should do.'

It was uncharacteristically modest of Hajdu to demote himself to a former 'assistant lecturer', having paraded his professorship in the *Daily Mail* the previous year. But his whimsical stunt was swiftly overtaken by events in Hungary itself, which were to propel Carl into almost every national newspaper in Britain.

...

To start at the end: the nemesis of Baron Carl Hajdu can be dated to 13 January 1957. From the moment the *Sunday Pictorial* reached the news-stands that morning, he knew the game was up. Alongside a photograph of a dapper, moustachioed character (captioned merely 'The Baron'), it carried the following story by Comer Clarke:

A flat-finding agent who claims to be a baron admitted last night: 'I have collected £2,000 for Hungarian relief, BUT – I am afraid I am going to have some difficulty in showing in the balance how it was spent.'

Pale, blue-eyed Hungarian-born 'Baron' Carl Hajdu, 37 – it is a Hungarian title, he says – runs the Apartment Lessors' Association, of Edgware Road, Paddington London.

When the Hungarians rose against the Reds last November he organised the Hungarian Freedom Fighters' Assistance Committee. In two days he raised £2,000 to send a contingent of English 'freedom fighters' to help the Hungarians. Scores of eager young men volunteered. But no 'freedom fighters' went to Hungary.

'As things turned out they could have done very little in the face of ferocious Russian oppression,' said Hajdu. 'I was told in any case that the sending of volunteers could cause diplomatic embarrassment.'

He added: '£1,500 was spent on helping Hungarian Freedom Fighters inside Hungary. About £500 of that went on expenses.'

I asked: 'Did you have an understanding with any official body about taking the money out of the country?'

Hajdu replied: 'I don't think I can answer that... I ought to speak to a friend of mine who's concerned with all this. I'm not much of a businessman. But my conscience is clear.'

Hajdu said £500 was given to refugees after arriving in this country. 'A balance sheet will be published soon by an accountant,' he said. 'About 400 people subscribed as a result of publicity. I have taken only out-of-pocket expenses. In less than two months I have been to Germany four times to help refugees.

'I am afraid we could never get anyone into Hungary. Or anyone out. We could help them only when they were over the border in Austria. We had a small committee to run affairs, but I was the boss since I know all about Hungary.'

Before describing the events that led to this unwelcome exposure, we might pause to consider Carl's state of mind. During his early years in England he had hoped to become a man of letters, but that ambition had been put aside after his marriage. Instead, he had begun to see himself as a successful businessman. While aspiring to the rewards, however, he was unwilling to put in the hard work. Where was the excitement, where the glory? The decision to throw himself into the Hungarian campaign was prompted by more than patriotism or anti-Communism – though no doubt those motives were genuine enough. He craved attention, status and applause. Here was an opportunity to make his reputation.

News of the anti-Soviet uprising in Budapest had begun to filter through on Wednesday 23 October 1956. On the Saturday, many Hungarians in London gathered at Mindszenty House in Notting Hill. Refugees were now streaming out of their native land, and – as refugees themselves – they were determined to help. A young man named Lajos Keppe protested that it was not the fugitives who needed assistance but those who stayed behind to fight. Carl spoke to him afterwards, and agreed to compose a circular letter soliciting money and materials. Twelve thousand copies were sent to people whose names they took from *Who's Who*, the classified phone book and the Catholic Directory. Such was the strength of feeling in Britain on behalf of Hungary that hundreds of cheques arrived at Carl's little office in the Edgware Road over the next 48 hours – as well as a long queue of well-wishers. A bank account was hastily opened, and a newly qualified accountant called Ted Freeman-Attwood offered to keep track of the money.

On Sunday 4 November, as the self-styled chairman of the UK Committee for the Assistance of Hungarian Freedom Fighters, Baron Hajdu led a mass march from the Brompton Oratory to 10 Downing Street, where a petition was handed in. The same day, contrary to their undertaking, the Russian army launched an attack against Budapest. Carl convened a press conference at his Chelsea flat the following morning. Describing himself as 'a former officer in the Hungarian army', he announced that 500 people in Britain had already volunteered to go and join the underground resistance. 'One applicant, who telephoned the London headquarters yesterday, is a young woman in a travel agency in York who says that she is a crack shot and is prepared to pay her own fare,' the *Manchester Guardian* reported. According to Hajdu, she and others would travel to the Continent as tourists, and then collect weapons promised by 'a high official source' before slipping across the border into the forests of western Hungary. No reporter was bold enough to ask how a small-time Paddington estate agent came to have such impressive top-level connections, or such easy access to hidden arsenals. 'This money is for a different purpose from the donations which other organisations are turning over to the Red Cross,' he told the *Guardian*. 'Those funds are going to buy warm pants for babies; this is to buy battledress for men. We are out to buy guns, not bandages.'

All Baron Hajdu's extravagant proclamations were treated as gospel. The *Daily Mail* praised this '36-year-old Hungarian exile whose call to action has brought support from many parts of Britain'. The *Evening News* interviewed one of his volunteers, 'pretty 22-year-old schoolteacher Jacqueline Watkinson', who would soon be leaving for 'a secret destination in Europe' and felt confident that long experience of pheasant-shooting with her father would enable her to repel the Reds. The paper added that 'the 36-year-old Baron, a former lecturer in English at Budapest University, says he knows of 1,500 people like Miss Watkinson. They all want to be guerrillas. And some day soon, he hopes, Miss Watkinson will be able to exchange her brown and black check blouse for the khaki clothes she will wear in the forests of Hungary.'

Cloak-and-dagger assignations, political passion – and pretty girls too. No wonder the newspapers loved the story. Their glee intensified when Jacqueline's father, Major Charles Watkinson, declared on the front page of the *News Chronicle* that he was shocked by his daughter's desire to take on the Russian army. It was like a spy novel, but for real. The Baron even implied that he would be joining the struggle himself. 'I and some friends are shortly taking a "holiday", and we shall just happen to arrive in Hungary,' he told a mass meeting of London students on 8 November. 'If anyone else wants to take a similar "holiday" I am sure it can be done and that what luggage you need will be provided.' And he may have meant it. Among the Home Office files at the Public Record Office in London is an 'application for a travel document by a foreign person unable to obtain a national passport', filled out by Carl Hajdu of 10 Cadogan Gardens on 12 November 1956. The countries he proposes to visit are listed as Austria, West Germany, Italy, France, Spain and Holland; the purpose of the journey is 'visiting friends, business negotiations'; and he wishes to leave in the 'next few days'. Two days later, to be precise: on 14 November he flew to Germany, accompanied by Lajos Keppe, to establish contact with Hungarian exiles in Frankfurt and Munich.

Scotland Yard, which had been observing Carl's antics closely, chose this moment to sabotage his campaign. During his absence, two detectives visited the Edgware Road offices and advised the young English volunteers to get out 'for their own good', rather than jeopardise their futures by associating with such a shady character. Hajdu's fresh-faced recruits were shocked. What had he done? The police declined to specify, but vague allusions to 'possible fraud' were enough to provoke a mass exodus of county girls, fearful for their families' reputations.

With Ted Freeman-Attwood the police were more frank, admitting that the suggestion of financial skulduggery was an excuse to suppress Carl's political activities. It would, they said, be highly embarrassing for the government if British subjects went to Hungary and got themselves killed by the Russians. Besides, the raising of a private army was illegal in England, however popular the cause. By tarnishing the baron's name, they hoped to avoid the political rumpus that might ensue if they tried to stop his crusade officially.

Freeman-Attwood resigned as treasurer, leaving Carl and Phyllis as sole signatories to the bank account, and the other committee members hastily signed a statement 'disassociating ourselves with anything undertaken by or in the name of the above committee from this day on… or from any undertakings which may be taking place or may have taken place without our knowledge or approval'. By the time Carl returned from Germany, his troops had all deserted. Their general received the *coup de grâce* from the *Sunday Pictorial* a few weeks later.

To the journalists who descended on Cadogan Gardens, Carl maintained a pose of heroic innocence. 'I have to consult tomorrow a highly placed civil servant,' he told the *Daily Sketch*. 'It would embarrass him if I spoke now – and I gave an undertaking that whatever I did to help Hungary would be done discreetly, so as not to embarrass the British government... A balance sheet showing how the money was spent will be sent to the Home Secretary soon.' It was a courageous performance from a man who was, in truth, plummeting into despair. Mr Theo, his landlord at the Edgware Road office, noticed that the baron's old confidence and exuberance had disappeared: he 'avoided your eyes like a shifty fox'.

In the spring of 1957 Carl and Phyllis were evicted from the Chelsea house for non-payment of rent, and moved steeply downmarket to a tiny flat in Dartmouth Park, Highgate. Meanwhile, a Hungarian named Alice Kresner, who had asked Carl to manage her properties while she was in Australia, returned to London and began pressing for the £350 he owed her. In July 1957, weary of his excuses, she applied to have him declared bankrupt. It is unusual for a private individual to go to such lengths, especially when there is no prospect of retrieving the debt, but Mrs Kresner's declared intention was that he should never again be entrusted with other people's money.

The bankruptcy order, which was granted in October, listed no fewer than 26 creditors, including the grand department store Harrods – a reminder of those recklessly hospitable evenings in Cadogan Gardens. And a visit by the bailiffs revealed just how little remained: his wristwatch raised £2, his fridge £20. All the worldly goods of Baron Hajdu were worth only £60. He then had to face the shame of a Public Examination, at which he again claimed to have no income beyond occasional gifts from his mother. Asked why his bank statements showed no such receipts, he said that she always sent English banknotes. His replies to questions about the Hungarian committee were even more evasive. The hearings were eventually adjourned *sine die*, meaning that he could never be discharged until he submitted satisfactory accounts.

One Saturday evening a few weeks before his bankruptcy the fire brigade arrived at the Apartment Lessors' Association in Edgware Road, summoned by a neighbour who smelt smoke. The blaze had been started by a gas ring in the back room and then spread to the floor below. Carl was taken to hospital suffering from burns to his hands and face. Although the police ruled out arson, Mr Theo had his doubts – particularly when he found a half-empty can of paraffin in the office. What had Carl been doing in the office on a Saturday night anyway? He may have been trying to destroy papers; or, indeed, to destroy himself. One of his future incarnations, Michael Karoly, was to write: 'Men were looking into the fire, not for what they might see in the flames, but to blind themselves with its brightness.'

He can hardly be blamed for wishing to avert his eyes from reality: the freedom-fighting hero of Fleet Street stood exposed as a disreputable failure, a grubby little thief who couldn't even support his wife and stepson. A later 'case history', in which Michael Karoly describes a client stricken with impotence, has a strongly auto-biographical resonance:

His mind was too preoccupied with his trouble in the office and he did not respond to [his wife's] advances. The harder he tried the more panicky he became. She was angry at first, then she started jeering. As she said: 'Oh, you're use-less, you're no good for anything...' He had fought his way up in the world, had achieved a good position, yet he was a failure as a man. He went to sleep that night brooding over it. He tried on several occasions to resume normal sexual relations with his wife, but each time he failed.

How did Carl deal with this humiliation? Once again, Michael Karoly provides the answer. In his book *Hypnosis*, published in 1961, Karoly wrote of the liberation experienced by a transvestite (or 'eonist', named after the cross-dressing Chevalier D'Eon) when he shrugs off man's attire:

He even thinks of himself as a woman, and in fact assumes another personality... This complete change of mental viewpoint creates a door through which the eonist can step into a nicer, more refined life, where his own feelings of inadequacy, originating in his lack of sexual vigour, are left behind with his manly personality. When he is a man he is, unlike the homosexual, masculine with all his manly virtues and shortcomings. When he is a woman he is the woman of his ideals, free of the grime of everyday life.

The eonist rarely wants to be cured. His activities are rather like the savoury before the meal whetting the appetite but never satisfying the hunger. The pleasures he experiences are exquisite because of the relief he feels from his constant insoluble problems, but he pays for them with remorse and distress which increase his craving.

Cynthia Holmes-Brand, who was lodging with the Hajdus, recalls that during the crises of 1957 Carl took his suitcase of women's clothes – including a pair of falsies and some stiletto-heeled shoes – out of storage at Harrods. If anyone asked, he said, she should pretend that they belonged to her. Soon afterwards he turned up at the Harley Street consulting room of the Canadian hynotherapist W. G. Warne-Beresford, complaining of 'nervous problems'.

Carl Hajdu's aspirations had been comprehensively thwarted. Very well then: he would find new aspirations – and 'another personality' which could embody them. Having approached Warne-Beresford as a patient, he soon enrolled as one of the hypnotherapist's pupils under the name of Michael B. Karoly.

Chapter Three

'We are all animals'

Michael B. Karoly was a far more dashing character than Carl Hajdu, with a taste for pork-pie hats, dark glasses and fast cars. From time to time he would affect a goatee beard to give himself a more intellectual air and, perhaps, to foil his transvestite urges. Having been christened Karoly Mihaly, he simply reversed the names and anglicised one. The middle initial stood for Blaise, an exotic embellishment of his own devising. English people had always struggled with the pronunciation of 'Hajdu': Karoly was much easier, while still strange enough to arouse curiosity. It had aristocratic echoes, too: Count Michael Karolyi had been a famous Hungarian statesman after the First World War.

To qualify for membership of Warne-Beresford's organisation, the British Society of Hypnotherapists, trainees had to study for a year and then sit an exam in 'anatomy, physiology, biology, neurology and practical hypnotherapy'. The results of Michael's class can be found in the *Times* of 5 September 1958; his name is not among the successful candidates, but this didn't deter him from using the initials M.B.S.H. and touting for business. He placed an advertisement in the *Hendon Times*: 'Anxiety, blushing, nervous tension, lack of self-confidence, personal problems, treated by hypnosis by qualified psychologist, graduate of eminent Continental University. For new appointments phone (only 6.30-8pm) Gulliver 1453.' One of his first clients was Dorothy Shirley, a matronly Jewish author in her late fifties who wrote short stories for the *Lady*, *Tribune* and John O'London's *Weekly* as well as typing manuscripts for the novelists Kingsley Amis and John Fowles. However bogus his claims to be 'qualified' as a psychologist or hypnotist, Mrs Shirley seems to have been a thoroughly satisfied customer – so much so that she sent him a poem which was used later as a preface to his book on hypnotism:

> Your voice said 'Sleep!' With mind awake
> I slept. You bade my spirit take
> Comfort from that sleep. I slept.

The words flowed through my soul: I kept
Their cadence and their meaning fast
Against my grief until, as last,
In waking, silent trance, I saw
A vision which, without a flaw,
Filled me with light that softly lay
Beyond the touch of night or day.

Few of his clients are now traceable. Only one is certain that he was successfully hypnotised: Michael performed the party trick of making the man lie across three chairs and then removing the middle one. Another recalls being instructed to raise his right arm; to this day he doesn't know whether he was in a genuine trance or whether he obeyed so as not to disappoint Michael. But all felt that their money – £5 a session – had been well spent. Michael had a talent for putting people at their ease, using relaxation and breathing techniques as a prelude to hypnosis. In 1967, when he practised only exceptionally, a patient was referred to him by a doctor at New Park hospital, Epsom, so at least one qualified psychiatrist must have had confidence in his talents.

'A man who has no doubts in his mind about his ability to hypnotise people is a good hypnotist,' Michael wrote. 'He is a man of great self-assurance.'

Whatever his shortcomings, he certainly never lacked for self-assurance: to each of his various identities he brought the unwavering authenticity of a great method actor. Which may explain why, in 1959, he offered his services as a psychology lecturer to the Stanislavsky Studio in Knightsbridge, the London counterpart of the more famous Actors' Studio in New York.

As an unnaturalised alien, he still had to inform the police of any change of occupation: his official certificate of registration shows that by September that year he was describing himself proudly as 'author, consultant, lecturer'. In his Stanislavsky seminars, which were more like group therapy sessions, he made no distinction between male and female students and encouraged each to take the others' parts. (After hours, he was most interested in the girls – sometimes rather more so than the rules of the Studio allowed.) In an unfinished essay on Stanislavsky, perhaps anticipating future objections to Charlotte Bach, Michael noted that 'like all great innovators, he did not invent anything, only discovered the obvious. What he said was self-evident and, as is usual with such things, it came to be regarded as revolutionary.'

As Michael began to discover, there is always a ready market for statements of the obvious if they are dressed up as specialist knowledge. No one would have paid for the psychological insights of an unsuccessful flat-agent from Paddington, but after acquiring an arsenal of bogus qualifications – 'Michael B. Karoly, Sc.Sc. (Budapest), D.Psy, C.P.E. (Cantab), MBSH', his writing-paper now boasted – he suddenly found himself in demand as a man with something to say. After meeting Michael at a party in the autumn of 1960, the literary agent Peter Tauber recommended him to the features editor of *Today*, a weekly general-interest magazine, and by the following January he was a regular contributor – billed as '*Today*'s psychological expert'. He seemed able to turn his hand to anything: 'My Frank Advice to Eva' (the divorce of Eva Bartok), 'Should Big Girls be Spanked?' (disciplining teenage daughters), 'Is This Man a Brute?' (baby-battering fathers) and 'Why Oh Why Do I Steal?' (shoplifting). Thanks to Peter Tauber, a fellow émigré from Hungary, Michael was also commissioned to write a short paperback for the publisher Paul Elek – yet another Hungarian – which would explain hypnotism to a general audience. Working with commendable speed on his new Olivetti portable typewriter, he finished the manuscript in time for publication in September 1961. He and Phyllis celebrated the arrival of the publisher's advance by moving to a large flat in

Langbourne Mansions, a mock-Tudor block on the south side of Highgate Hill with panoramic views over London. Apart from a two-year exile in the West End during the mid-1960s, Langbourne Mansions remained Michael's home for the rest of his life.

Hypnosis, which appeared under the imprint of Elek's 'Bestseller Library', had admiring if brief reviews. ('Intelligent and balanced... most readable... easy for the layman to follow.') For those few people who knew Michael Karoly, however, some of the assembled 'case histories' must have sounded strangely familiar. Interviewed by the Scottish *Sunday Mail*, the 'former lecturer at Budapest University' observed that 'people can produce the solution to most of their own problems. The trouble is that so many of us run away from difficulties.' In Michael's case, he distanced himself from problems by attributing them to others. In both *Today* and the women's supplement of the *Daily Mirror* he had already written about shoplifters; now there was a further lengthy instalment in the book, accurately summarised by the *Mail* thus:

A man in trouble told a hypnotist: 'I can't help stealing things and taking them home.' It was one of the most unusual cases ever to come before psychologist Michael Karoly. Quiet-voiced Karoly, an exiled Hungarian, uses hypnotism in his flourishing practice. But what could he do for a man like this?

Randolph was the patient's name. He was 42, a university graduate. But he couldn't resist stealing things – articles that he wanted for himself. He never sold them. He took them home.

His haul included a bundle of library books. Mysteriously most of the things he had taken seemed to be owned by the government or a local council. Hypnosis provided the answer. In a trance he admitted that he felt 'society owed me these things'.

He had worked for a public charity that began to go bankrupt. To try to save it, he had ploughed in money of his own. But it still collapsed. And instead of being thanked, gossips hinted that he had bungled the funds. Unconsciously, stealing was his way of hitting back.

Hypnotism made him face his moment of truth. Karoly quietly told him it was time to face facts. Randolph suddenly called to tell him that he now realised two wrongs could never make a right.

He was cured. And he has never stolen since.

Michael Karoly was now 41, not 42, but in every other respect he is here rewriting history to his own advantage. Once again he awards himself (or the non-existent 'Randolph') a university degree; in the saga of the freedom-fighters' committee he emerges as victim rather than villain. The final paragraph is a lovely self-exculpatory flourish: in reality, Michael – and then Charlotte – continued to steal books from Highgate library for many more years. By 'curing' his fictional patient, an incorrigible fantasist transformed himself into the dispenser of truth. A few months later the *Hampstead & Highgate Express* reported that 'psychologist Michael Karoly' wished to interview shoplifters in the hope of discovering why they steal – an odd ambition, given that he seemed to know the answer already. As he told the paper, 'I estimate that one person in five has stolen from a store at one time or another. Most of them, of course, are not criminals, neither are they basically dishonest. They steal during times of emotional stress in response to some sudden temptation.'

• • •

In his unpublished autobiographical novel *Siobhan*, Michael mentions that although he no longer uses his baronial title, his wife does so 'with great gusto. She has a separate telephone line with her name, complete with title, in the directory. That's all right with me, as long as I am not involved. She says it is useful in her business.' Sure enough, in the London phone-books for July 1963 and October 1964, Phyllis is listed as 'Hajdu, Baroness P.M., 81 Langbourne Mansions...' (Michael Karoly has a different number at the same address.) After a spell as a bookkeeper for a trade union she had by then entered a business better suited to her social aspirations, working at a Mayfair gallery which specialised in Chinese art and antiques. 'In her job Phyllis did come into contact with the uppermost levels of society,' he wrote. 'Even though very junior as an art expert, her pleasing personality made her liked by almost everyone. Members of the Royal Family and many of the richest sections of the peerage would ask for her by name in the dealing with the firm.' Colleagues at the gallery remember that it was Phyllis who sought out the toffs rather than vice versa: she put on 'all sorts of airs and graces', and boasted of having been a weekend guest of the Marquess of Bath at Longleat.

Though few believed her, this tall story did have a very slight foundation of truth. In April 1962 Michael had written to the Marquess's son, Lord Weymouth, proposing a meeting. 'My name may not be altogether unknown to you,' he began, rather optimistically. 'I am

Clockwise from top left: Karoly, Vilma, Tibor and their parents; portrait of Karoly as a young spiv in wartime Budapest; Michael with unknown companion at the World Wildlife Fund ball, June 1964; at 10 Downing Street, 28 October 1956

Right: The transformation – a composite photo of Michael with his new 'sister', Charlotte, 1965

Above: Phyllis at her flat in Langbourne Mansions, Highgate...which provided the backdrop for many self-portraits of Michael trying on his late wife's clothes after her death in 1965 *(See left and following pages)*

Above:
Charlotte
being fitted
for a new wig,
c.1970

Right: Lecturing
in London,
c.1975

an established author, journalist and lecturer on matters appertaining to psychology. At present I am engaged in collecting material for a book in which I intend to convey the contemporary British scene. In connection with this I would be very interested in having your views on various aspects of life.' Karoly added that although he contributed regularly to magazines such as *Today* and *Woman's Mirror*, 'I am not contemplating the use of this material in articles for those publications. If by any chance I wanted to do so in the unforeseeable future, please accept my assurances that I shall be seeking your permission in advance.'

Later in the 1960s Lord Weymouth became famous as 'the hippy peer', a bearded eccentric who painted erotic murals and maintained a harem of 'wifelets'. In 1962, however, he was a reclusive figure, largely unknown to the public. Understandably wary, he decided to check the qualifications listed on Michael Karoly's writing paper: Cambridge University had no graduate of that name; nor was he registered with the British Psychological Society. The discovery strengthened Weymouth's misgivings, but also stimulated his curiosity. He invited Karoly to lunch.

Although the pretext for contacting Weymouth had been a desire to hear his opinions, it was Michael who dominated the conversation. He spent several hours trying to persuade the young peer of the benefits of psychoanalysis; more worryingly, from his host's point of view, he spoke of the need for wealthy aristocrats to invest in business ventures. 'There seems quite a possibility that Mr Karoly is a confidence trickster out to hook me,' Weymouth noted in his diary. 'The man is a pest... I am doubtful if he was really interested in me as a person, rather than as a potential financial asset.' Alternatively, he surmised, Karoly might have a psychological problem of his own: a desperate longing for contact with the upper classes. This suspicion, aroused when Michael began boasting about his own Hungarian barony, was confirmed a few days later when the William Hickey column of the *Daily Express* reported Weymouth's 'cooperation' with the psychologist.

Mr Karoly, a Highgate consultant who studied at Budapest University, is compiling the first psychological analysis of the peerage, which he will publish as a book. His aim: to find out what the peers think of themselves and what they think other people are thinking about them. His method: heart-to-heart interviews in the homes of as many as he can lay hands on.

'My theory is that most of them suffer from aristocracy neurosis,' says 42-year-old Mr Karoly, author of a recent book on hypnosis and psychotherapy. 'Fundamentally, they feel on the defensive against a hostile world which they believe regards them as odd. They also lack incentive, a vital factor in our lives, for there is little left for them to achieve.

'Emotionally they are probably the least stable section of the community. They shut themselves up in their castles too much. They should mix more.'

So much for Michael's promise that there would be no publicity without the consent of his subjects. Weymouth, indignant at the betrayal, became even angrier later that morning when the postman delivered a copy of *Hypnosis* by Michael Karoly and a magnificently patronising letter from the author. 'What you don't seem to realise,' Karoly informed the peer, 'is that, as you are at the moment, you are progressively reducing your contact with the outside world to those who fit in with your preconceptions. This way your misconceptions are merely being reinforced instead of eliminated. And believe me, you have plenty of misconceptions. This will inevitably lead to mental and emotional sterility, or in other words to artistic suicide. That however is your problem, not mine. I can give you useful pointers how to achieve your salvation, but I cannot do it for you.' Quite so: Weymouth decided that he'd save his own soul rather than entrust it to 'a fat old gas-bag who seems to think he has the qualities of a messiah', and wrote to Karoly telling him so. 'I notice,' he added, 'that my name has already been mentioned in the press in relation to your work. This was in direct contravention of your written assurances. I wish you luck in your venture, but for my own part I prefer to retain my privacy in these matters.'

Had Michael been capable of shame or embarrassment he might have accepted the rebuke in guilty silence. Instead, characteristically, he adopted a pose of baffled and injured innocence: 'I would like to point out most emphatically that I did not in any way discuss with them our recent meeting. Indeed I referred to it only in the vaguest possible terms.' Happily oblivious to the contradiction between the second sentence and the first, he continued: 'If it is any consolation to you, I also suffered a great deal by the publication of this piece of writing. It was inaccurate on more than one point and it was most certainly premature beyond measure… At our meeting I felt that our acquaintance might have developed into an intellectually fertile friendship.' Weymouth did not reply. ('I'm not going to let him get his foot in the door a second time,' he wrote in his diary. 'Once was quite enough.') And Phyllis never had her visit to Longleat.

In August 1962 Michael compiled a quiz for *Today*

which invited wives to answer the question: 'Do You Really Love Your Husband?' He suggested that some women silently and slowly grow to hate their husbands without even realising it. This is yet another example of his tendency to generalise from his own private pre-occupations, since the marriage to Phyllis was indeed disintegrating. In their early years together there had often been rows, but these always ended in fond reconciliation; now, however, he preferred to remain silent when she turned on him. Phyllis confided to a friend that her husband's charms were all for show and that he was impotent in bed. He was also a remarkably inattentive stepfather: in his many autobiographical essays and novels about this period, Peter is scarcely mentioned. The boy had grown up into a desperately shy teenager who rarely ate with his family and, if he spoke at all, was monosyllabic.

Later that year Michael started renting a small flat at 23 Hertford Street, London W1, in the shadow of the newly built Hilton Hotel. Intended only as a consulting room, whose Mayfair address might impress prospective clients, the flat soon became a more permanent refuge where he could escape from Phyllis's chiding and indulge his fantasies. The following story turns up in one of Michael's 'case histories':

I used to keep my gear [i.e. women's clothes] in the office and sometimes, after a hard week, I would go in over the weekend pretending to do some urgent work. I would dress up and just lounge around for a few hours. It is impossible to describe the effect it had on me. A week's Mediterranean cruise or a month of golfing at St Andrews isn't a patch on it.

Once I had a rather bad year. Nothing seemed to go right. Bills were piling up and money wasn't coming in. On paper I was doing very well, yet every time rent day or the phone bill came it was a major disaster. That's when I went out for the first few times. I used to get dressed in the office, put my shirt, tie, jacket and trousers on top, dash to the car and drive to a town 40-50 miles away. In a quiet spot I would stop, take off the top clothes, put my wig and high-heeled shoes on, make up and generally make myself presentable. Then I would drive into the town as a lady from the shire on a shopping trip...

The 'client' is eventually arrested when a passer-by guesses his secret and complains to the police. One would be tempted to dismiss this as another Karoly fiction, were it not for a news item that appeared in the *Hertfordshire Mercury* on 26 April 1963:

MAN DRESSED AS WOMAN WALKS INTO HOTEL

A man dressed completely in female clothing walked into a Hertford hotel on Good Friday, and was later arrested as he drove – still dressed as a woman – to Knebworth, it was stated at Hertford court on Thursday of last week.

Before the court was Carl Michael Blaise Augustine Hajdu, of 81 Langbourne Mansions, Holly Lodge, Highgate, London. He was charged with conduct likely to cause a breach of the peace.

He pleaded guilty and agreed to be bound over in the sum of £10 to keep the peace for a year. He was ordered to pay four shillings costs.

Inspector E. W. Pegg, prosecuting, said that Hajdu walked into an hotel and went up to the first floor flat of the landlord and his family. He asked if he could change.

'He was completely dressed in female attire,' said the inspector, who handed a photograph of Hajdu to the magistrates.

The incident was reported to Hertford police and later Hajdu was found driving a car on the way to Knebworth. He was detained.

In the fictional version, 'John' too has himself charged under an old name by which few people know him. 'But one person knew me by both names,' he tells the psychologist. 'My wife. I couldn't take the chance of her finding out. Or, to be more precise, I couldn't have faced her if I had. I walked out, leaving her a note that I was fed up with marriage and wanted to live it up while still fairly young. I figured this would hurt her less than the truth. I don't know if I did right or wrong. She never found out the real reason. She died in an accident a year later. Did I love her? After 20 years you don't love your wife. You just don't want to live apart from her. I felt I had to.'

Michael moved into the Mayfair flat full-time, ready to 'live it up', even if loneliness and remorse often drew him back to Highgate at weekends for Sunday lunch with Phyllis. And, as ever, he sought to profit from adversity, this time by founding a therapy group called Divorcees Anonymous: though not actually divorced himself, he now felt qualified to advise others – for a fee – on how to deal with the financial problems of setting up a new household, the divided loyalties of friends and the pain of deserted children.

The literary agent Peter Tauber went to a Divorcees Anonymous meeting at Michael's flat, and was appalled by what he saw: two dozen women, all in an emotionally vulnerable state, most of whom appeared to be besotted with their host. But the journalist Nancy Banks-Smith, another visitor, was profoundly impressed. In the *Daily Express* of 3 August 1963 she wrote a long, admiring feature about Divorcees Anonymous – 'the idea of London psychologist Michael Karoly, who found that introducing divorced or separated people to each other worked wonders'. It certainly worked wonders for Michael, who had already seduced several of the members.

Eyeing up attractive women was like a nervous twitch with him: he couldn't resist giving them what he called his 'undressing look'. While idly enjoying this disconcerting pastime in one of his favourite Mayfair pubs on a summer's day in 1963, he first noticed the woman he came to regard as the love of his life. Much of what follows is taken from the novel he wrote about his affair with Siobhan (not her real name, for reasons that will become apparent), and may not always be the literal truth; but insofar as details can be checked – when, for instance, they allude to actual events and people – he seems to have been mostly accurate. Certainly there is no reason to doubt the *amour fou* which seized him that lunchtime in the Shepherd's Tavern:

He strode with firm steps towards the door, keeping his eyes on her all the time. Until then her face had only half turned towards him. Whether it was accidental or perhaps an unconscious urge on her part to have a better look at him, she now abruptly turned her whole body, facing him almost squarely in his path.

They looked into each other's eyes. At that moment an extraordinarily solid contact formed between them. In his mind's eye, all her clothes fell off and she was standing there naked and proud, with powerful hips, firm breasts; their arms wrapped around each other. He knew with an almost mystical certainty that her eyes too stripped him naked, experiencing the same solid contact. As he came level with her, their eyes still firmly welded together, a great mushroom cloud exploded silently in his brain.

Two weeks later they were in bed – or, rather, making do with cushions on the floor. Their first date may have been a slap-up meal in Trader Vic's at the Hilton, but Michael hadn't yet made the down payment on a bed for the Hertford Street rooms. He bought one very soon afterwards, as an urgent necessity. In his novel, she is described as 'a big healthy sturdy peasant girl' – though actually she was the daughter of a minor peer, a fact which gave her snobbish lover a delicious thrill. Someone else who met her described Siobhan as a fat, masculine loud-mouth. Maybe that was the attraction: having been wretchedly impotent with the classy and ultra-feminine Phyllis, he found to his amazement that with earthy Siobhan he could make love for hours. But it wasn't just sex; his account of their post-coital conversations is peppered with phrases such as 'spiritual ecstasy' and 'mystical oneness', and extravagant philosophical fancies:

> The word love sounded not only inadequate but phoney. He knew that this was something else. It was as if he'd caught a glimpse of a philosophical abyss, revealing the deepest roots of Nature's life force. The same primeval urge which forced the amoeba to stop propagating by dividing itself and go in search of a mate, seeking out the myriads of life forms at the bottom of the primordial sea, the one which was its own kind... Now another thought emerged at the back of his mind. Wild animals in the zoo. Refusing to mate out of their natural element. Was Siobhan his natural element?

Within weeks of their first naked grapple, however, Michael was trying to end the affair. At 24, Siobhan was almost 20 years his junior, and despite all the primordial passion – or perhaps because of it – he could see no future for them. Nor did their sublime, mystical oneness inhibit him from pursuing short-lived affairs with several of the women from Divorcees Anonymous while she was away in the country visiting her parents at weekends. Having rediscovered his sexual prowess, he was eager to bestow it widely.

In the autumn of 1963 a young man turned up at the consulting rooms in Hertford Street, saying that he had heard of Divorcees Anonymous and would like to attend a meeting before deciding whether to join. Unlike other newcomers, who were usually pretty diffident at first, he had no hesitation in asking many searching questions about love, marriage and adultery – and about the organisation's funds. The following Sunday morning, while taking a leisurely bath, Michael heard an odd noise from the office-cum-sitting-room. Someone had thrown a copy of the *People*, a mass-circulation scandal-sheet, through the open window. At the top of an inside page was a snatched photo of Michael next to the headline: 'The Strange Facts About "Divorcees Anonymous"… and the Bashful Mr K. Who Runs It.' The inquisitive young man, *People* reporter Derek Ive, must have taken copious notes throughout the session, or have been possessed of a most retentive memory:

Mr Karoly wasted no time in beginning the treatment. 'Tell

me,' he snapped at a new member visiting the club for the first time, 'was sexual incompatibility the cause of your divorce? Will you tell us about it?' The woman, obviously embarrassed, evaded the question by changing the subject.

Mr Karoly then delivered a lecture on fidelity in marriage. He suggested that adultery by a man was less important than the unfaithfulness of a wife. And he declared: 'Sex is the most important thing. We must remember that really we are only animals.'

Some of the well-dressed 'animals' listening looked distinctly uncomfortable, especially one woman who had told me that she came from a titled family.

At the end of the meeting Mr Karoly suggested that everyone should adjourn to a nearby pub and led the way, leading an attractive young divorcee by the arm. I didn't have the heart to tell the bemused club members that so controversial are Mr Karoly's methods that they have actually caused a divorce… a section of the club has found its views incompatible with those of Mr K. and has set up a rival organisation.

The more sensitive of them couldn't stand Mr Karoly's habit of reading aloud from personal letters he had received. 'I was shocked,' said a member of the breakaway group. 'I joined Divorcees Anonymous for companionship. I never expected to hear extracts from someone else's sex life. Mr

Karoly read out intimate details from letters written by members. We knew who the members were – which made it very embarrassing.'

Michael read all this with a weary sense of déjà vu. The committee for Hungarian freedom-fighters and the Apartment Lessors' Association had both fallen victim to Sunday newspaper exposés, and now history was repeating itself – even down to the allegations of financial malpractice. 'When Divorcees Anonymous was formed,' one of the disgruntled ex-members told the paper, 'Mr Karoly said it was non-profit making, but he invited members to send a voluntary entrance fee of two guineas – and of course nearly everyone did. We had no treasurer and when we suggested the club be put on a proper basis Mr Karoly got rather annoyed. We wanted to form a committee, but he wouldn't have it.'

After quoting a condemnation of Divorcees Anonymous by the more respectable Marriage Guidance Council ('a club like this is a constant reminder of failure for the members'), Derek Ive delivered his *coup de grâce*: 'Yes, I think that if anyone needs advice from the Marriage Guidance council it is Mr Michael Karoly... who admits that his own marriage is on the rocks and that he and his wife are living apart.'

When Phyllis saw the article, she rang Michael and announced icily that there would no longer be a place for him at Sunday lunch. Soon afterwards, she began an affair with an American actor. Meanwhile, Siobhan at last accepted his suggestion that they separate – at the very moment when he was changing his mind, yearning for the comforts of her sturdy thighs.

Karoly was 43 and alone in the world: his second adolescence had been sabotaged by the onset of a midlife crisis. He spent more and more time drinking in Mayfair pubs, observing resentfully that other men of his age or younger seemed to enjoy the financial and romantic success that eluded him. Yet he still strove to maintain the pose of a prosperous man-about-town, seeking out anyone who might offer useful introductions. One new acquaintance from the pub, a PR man called Richard Fulford-Brown, had agreed to back a charity ball for the newly formed World Wildlife Fund and invited Michael to join the committee.

Charity balls of this kind are a regular feature of the London scene, allowing well-heeled businessmen to parade their benevolent instincts while enjoying a lavish bun-fight and gratifying their social ambitions among a cast of guests straight out of *Burke's Peerage*. The patrons of the World Wildlife Fund event included the

Duchess of Westminster, the Earl of Bessborough, Lady Bicester, Lady Normanton and Lord Strathcarron – and, as the publicity leaflets revealed enticingly, 'HRH Princess Alexandra of Kent, GCVO, and the Hon. Angus Ogilvy have graciously consented to be present'. Michael had little to offer his smart new colleagues. At committee meetings he drank wine, smoked continuously and said almost nothing; some members wondered if he were on drugs. He made only one contribution to the preparations for the ball: on 23 May 1964 Lord Weymouth was surprised to receive a letter from the pestilential psychologist whom he had banished from Longleat two years earlier. 'I am fully aware that since our last encounter I cannot really count myself among your friends,' Michael wrote, with customary understatement. 'This, however, was your decision and I do not wish to influence you on that point. Now, however, I find myself one of the organisers of the World Wildlife Fund Ball... I wonder if you would be prepared to donate one of your paintings for the tombola. As you recall I have seen your paintings and I think they are far too good not to let others enjoy them too.' Flattery got him nowhere: it had clearly not occurred to Michael that the heir to Longleat regarded himself as a serious artist, working with a view to holding an exhibition one day, rather than an upper-class amateur whose pictures were fit only for tombola prizes. Weymouth declined to answer.

By then, however, Michael had another aristocrat in his web. At a cocktail party in the Dorchester Hotel for committee members, his eye had been caught by the elegant figure of Barbara, Marchioness of Lansdowne, one of the two joint-chairmen. She seems to have noticed him, too: after another reception a few days later, held at the Duke of Westminster's house in Brook Street, he escorted Lady Lansdowne back to her place in Charles Street and stayed the night.

Michael's excitement at seducing a genuine Marchioness – albeit one who was depressive and often drunk – is recorded in Pooterish detail in his novel *Siobhan*. Collecting her ladyship from a dinner party one evening, he was 'introduced to a minor member of the royal family!'.

The high point of his giddy social ascent was a visit to the theatre with an Austrian prince, an English viscount and a Belgian countess. Michael's breast swelled as they were shown to the best seats in the house. Afterwards, at Lady Lansdowne's, the Austrian prince even claimed to recognise his Hungarian title. The hostess, who knew about Siobhan, swiftly pricked the bubble of Michael's self-importance by implying that he was no more than a bit of rough she had picked up, a failed hypnotist whose wife and girlfriend had both deserted him. Furious at the slight, he walked out and never saw her again.

Seven months later, newspapers reported that the Marchioness of Lansdowne had died as a result of an accident with a 12-bore shotgun in the gunroom of her Scottish house. In his novel, Michael construed this as the suicide of a broken-hearted woman – while adding that he was no more to blame than a single drop of water in a full glass can be blamed for its eventual spilling over.

Besides, why torment himself about his possible responsibility for the Marchioness's death when he had more than enough problems of his own? Many clients of his hypnotherapy practice had shunned him since the *People* article appeared, and in the summer of 1964 he was given notice to quit the rooms in Hertford Street. Though he eventually found a small flat over a shop in Shepherd's Market, Mayfair, the search for new accommodation kept him away from the phone for long periods, and that was bad for business. After ditching the Marchioness, there were one or two brief love affairs that came to nothing: he was still obsessed with

Siobhan, concocting elaborate fantasies about how he might win her back. The announcement of her engagement in October 1964, published in the *Times*, hit him like a right uppercut, especially when he learned that her fiancé was divorced. It was the first of several shocks that were to precipitate the most serious crisis of his life. At Siobhan's wedding, held in Marylebone register office a few months later, he watched from across the street, unable to cry. He then returned to his flat in Shepherd's Market and wrote a 360-page novel in the hope of exorcising the grief.

Back in the summer of 1964 Phyllis had asked Michael to come back, but at that stage he was still holding out for Siobhan. Now he made the pilgrimage to Highgate, begging for forgiveness and reconciliation – only to find that his wife had recently taken up with a young man called David. She was also awaiting a gallstone operation and often seemed dazed, almost comatose. Phyllis told Michael that she and David were about to go on a motoring holiday in Germany with Peter, now studying architecture in Oxford, and his girlfriend, Judy Philpot. She would think about their marriage and let him know the verdict on her return.

Although she was on medication and had been ordered by her doctor not to drink, the Baroness Hajdu (as she still called herself) relaxed the rule a little during their tour of the Rhine valley. Then she became frighteningly ill and a mad rush back to England ensued. On the flight from Le Touquet her condition worsened; an ambulance was waiting as the plane landed at Lydd. Phyllis was rushed to Ashford hospital, accompanied by her son. She died of a 'severe uterine haemorrhage' two days later. Within a few weeks, Peter would also be dead.

Chapter Four

Death of a hypnotist

In later years, Charlotte Bach told a friend that the deaths of her 'husband' and son had been a kind of liberation. 'When it was over and they were both gone,' she said, 'despite all the trouble, in a funny sort of way it was a relief having that lot out of the way.' Although Michael's shock and grief were undoubtedly sincere, the bereavement also gave him the rare opportunity to become, however briefly, the focus of sympathy.

He therefore insisted on the most lavish and expensive funeral, held in Phyllis's home town of Pembroke Dock. He had the bill sent to the Welsh aunt who had looked after Peter in his early childhood – even though she had herself been widowed recently and was almost penniless. Understandably upset, she returned it to Michael. Soon afterwards, Peter visited his mother's employers at the

John Sparks gallery to seek condolences and, he hoped, an *ex gratia* payment. He found the place in turmoil. Phyllis had often turned up to work in new outfits which were said to be gifts from a generous 'sister' or 'cousin', but during her absence on holiday the truth had been discovered: she had systematically embezzled thousands of pounds. Stunned by the news of his mother's frauds, Peter soon made another shocking discovery: he was illegitimate. While going through her papers, he found that she had been granted a divorce from her first husband because of his inability to consummate the marriage.

Peter went back to the Oxford School of Architecture a week later, hoping to distract himself with study, while his stepfather returned to his own form of therapy – completing the novel *Siobhan*. 'The day I finished it in longhand,' he wrote, 'I phoned Peter in Oxford and asked him to have a meal with me as a celebration. It is impossible to explain how close we became to each other in those few days after Phyllis's death.' After lunching at Michael's local pub in Mayfair, Peter and his girlfriend Judy Philpot took the tube to Ruislip, where Judy's mother was visiting a relation. That evening Peter drove the two women back to Oxford in Mrs Philpot's Mini.

A Thame jury returned a verdict of accidental death yesterday on three young men who died as a result of a triple car crash on the A40 at Tetsworth last month [the *Oxford Mail* reported on 16 June 1965].

A man who saw the accident, Mr Campbell McLeod, said that just after midnight on Saturday 15 May a Triumph sports car 'travelling exceptoinally fast' had collided head-on with an Austin Mini while overtaking a Ford Zodiac. 'Suddenly there was an explosion and sparks like a firework display and a car came bouncing down the road towards me like a football,' he said.

The driver of the Mini, Mr Peter William Rodgers, a 20-year-old architectural student at Oxford, and the passenger of the Triumph, Mr Keith Charles Henderson, 19, a student of economic, were both killed instantly. The driver of the Triumph, Mr Ralph John Hanhart, 19, a trainee chartered surveyor, died as a result of his injuries.

Michael was at first mystified when the police knocked on his door. 'No, no,' he said, 'you've made a mistake. It was my wife who died, three weeks ago.' Two days later he applied to have his refugee passport renewed, explaining that he wished to travel to 'Spain, Italy, USA, some South American countries (at the moment I do not know which ones)… following the death of my wife and son'. In fact, however, he went no further than Phyllis's flat in Langbourne Mansions, where he shut himself away from the world – waking at three in the afternoon, watching television continuously until closedown, then returning to bed and reading trashy novels, works of philosophy or whatever else he could lay his hands on. With characteristic self-aggrandisement, he later suggested that these few weeks were his equivalent to Jesus's 40 days in the wilderness ('an archetypal shamanistic crisis') – and, as if that weren't enough, had elements of the crucifixion as well ('a consummatory shamanistic ecstasy, where the shaman dies and is reborn'). On rare excursions to the shops he walked with his head bowed, staring at the pavement and spurning any neighbours who tried to engage him in conversation.

He also bought himself an automatic camera. When Charlotte Bach died, her dressing-table drawers were found to be stuffed with dozens of photographs of the then Michael dressed in his wife's clothes, the earliest of which had been taken two months after Peter's death. Although Michael was far taller than Phyllis, her clothes magically seemed to fit; it was fortunate for him that the fashion in hemlines was rising. Studying these photo albums, one can see Michael rehearsing various female roles which he might now play. There is the ageing tart with the come-hither look, giving the camera an eyeful of her long legs (including the hairy thighs which peep out above her stocking-tops); the dutiful, domesticated hausfrau, forever ready with a brush and dustpan; and, rather more convincingly, the elegant and mature hostess, cigarette and wine-glass in hand as she awaits the guests' arrival at her sophisticated salon. Over the next few years he took many more photographs, through which one can follow Charlotte's gradual evolution. The startling black wig is succeeded by something greyer and less garish; the thighs are decorously hidden; the five o'clock shadow disappears beneath extra layers of make-up.

But the headaches of everyday existence could not be wished away. Camden Council, which owned Langbourne Mansions, refused to accept Michael as a legal tenant. In September 1965 he had the electricity account in Highgate transferred to his name, but the electricity board still pursued him for Phyllis's unpaid bill. That same month he was summonsed by Westminster Council for the overdue rates at his old flat in Mayfair. The phone company then joined the throng of creditors. And, to cap it all, the money left to him by Phyllis was running out. In March 1966 'Carl Hajdu' signed on at the labour exchange and began claiming National Assistance.

Michael's GP, Dr Wolynec, was worried enough to refer his increasingly strange patient to Richard Hunter's psychiatric clinic at the Whittington Hospital. 'He really is a very curious chap,' Hunter wrote to Wolynec. 'He has obviously got a good intelligence and knows how to look after himself, but, as you say, he has gone a bit dilapidated. Frankly, I do not think that he was ever self-supporting, but now that his wife's property is coming to an end, he has no other means of social assistance. Anyway, to start off with I think we ought to study him at close quarters and I have therefore arranged to admit him to one of my beds at Friern Hospital.'

Michael was well aware of the lure of madness. 'What petty bureaucrats don't realise – or don't want to realise – is how easy, how simple, how tempting it is to switch from one way of thinking to another,' he wrote in one of his notebooks. 'One is no longer restricted by what is reasonable, sensible, right or whatever meaning-less noise you care to call it... The madman has freed himself from all patterns.' He was less fanciful with his doctor at Friern Hospital. After Michael's discharge, Dr

Hunter wrote again to Dr Wolynec:

> This patient was admitted here from my Whittington
> Hospital outpatient clinic on 31/3/66 and stayed for a week.
> There is nothing very much wrong with him and I believe he
> is a bit of a sponger and suffers from a bit of pseudologia. He
> is anxious to have group treatment but I do not really know
> what for, and I do not think it will do any good, but I did say
> I would mention it to you. What he really ought to do is a reg-
> ular job of work before he becomes a rootless layabout. He is
> a man of good gifts, high intelligence and verbal facility and
> it would be a pity if these were allowed to act against him.

Michael claimed to have written three novels during
his long mourning. The first was *Siobhan* – which, with
breathtaking insensitivity, he despatched to the woman
who had inspired it, even though she was now happily
married to someone else. 'I thought you might as well
read it,' he explained. 'After all, it was written for you.
Not that it really matters any more. Since Peter's death I
am not the same person I used to be.' Siobhan and her
husband interpreted this as attempted blackmail. They
went straight to their solicitor, who wrote to warn
Michael that if he showed the 'libellous and obscene'
typescript to anyone else a libel writ would be issued.

The second novel (and the only other one which he seems to have completed) was *The Second Coming*, a science-fiction saga. 'I think I am becoming a woman,' Michael told a friend at the Stanislavsky Studio in 1966, and his plot summary for *The Second Coming* confirms that such metamorphoses were a growing pre-occupation:

A man falls in love with a girl. She becomes pregnant but prefers an abortion to marriage. The man has a sex-conversion operation, including the insertion of a womb, has the embryo transplanted and gives birth to a boy child. She brings him up as a good mother and the child grows up to be a talented, handsome young man. Then she meets a young woman and takes a great liking to her. The boy dies in an accident and...

One day, while writing this book, Michael had what felt like a minor epileptic fit, 'except that I was fully conscious'. Shivering and shaking, he fell to his knees and repeated several times: 'I hate my mother, I hate my father.' Since he didn't actually hate them at all, he brooded for days about what had possessed him to say such a thing, and concluded eventually that what he hated was 'father and mother archetypes' – and, more generally, the archetypes of male and female. Beside his novels, during this period Michael filled three notebooks with his thoughts, many on the possibility of transfiguration. 'I do not believe in evolution,' he wrote, 'and I do not believe in special creation. But I do believe in miracles, wrought spontaneously out of the inner substance of things. I would believe in God, if I were God.' Elsewhere in the notebooks he copied down passages from Vladimir Nabokov's *Lolita*, the story of a man with a dreadful obsession.

Gradually, Michael came to believe that the vicissitudes of his life, which had hitherto seemed no more than a 'meaningless tangle' – the sexual and financial disasters, the battles with officialdom – had their own complex pattern. If only he could discern its shape, he would know what to do next.

His persecutors were ready to assist, unwittingly, by precipitating yet another crisis. In May 1966 Michael was up before Bow Street magistrates charged with 13 offences of obtaining credit under false pretences and of carrying on trade as a psychologist under the name Michael B. Karoly without disclosing that as Carl Hajdu he was an undischarged bankrupt. His creditors included Frank Leverton, to whom he owed money for two expensive funerals, as well as the electricity board, the phone company and two shops. He was jailed for three months.

After serving his sentence at Ford open prison in Kent, Michael returned to Langbourne Mansions in radiant health: he had been working in the prison garden, where regular exercise and fresh air had done him a power of good. As a souvenir, he helped himself to a copy of the New Testament from the prison library. Five days after his release he placed an advert in *Queen* magazine: 'Professional gentleman, middle forties, widower, recently lost entire family, in need of new circle of friends, willing to act "the odd man" at dinner parties. Tall, presentable, reasonably civilised, adequately house-trained...' No one replied.

Despite his spell behind bars, Westminster Council still wanted its rates, and took him to court again that August. A dramatised account of the case in his notebooks, which probably owes more to imagination than to reality, exposes the intensity of his grudge against society:

MK to prosecuting counsel: Are you trying to send me back to jail? If so, I have no objection to it. I find the company there more congenial than bandying words with vermin like you.

Magistrate (surprised): What do you mean?

MK: There the criminals, most of them, only make a dishonest living out of other people's fortunes, while these gentlemen make a so-called honest living out of other people's misfortunes. I find this the more despicable...

Magistrate: Watch your tongue or I'll send you to jail!

MK: So you are admitting that prisons are not places where the wayward should make amends for his errors, but the means whereby the petty bourgeoisie can hit back in blind anger at those who refuse to play the game.

Magistrate: I am warning you again, you are in danger of being in contempt of court!

MK: Contempt of court? Are you being serious? Of course I have nothing but contempt for this... this farce. You can force me to attend and play your idiotic game, but you can't force me to respect this farce.

Michael was ordered to pay off Westminster Council at the rate of £1 a week, which even he could just about manage. Other problems, too, were sorting themselves out. Camden Council finally agreed to accept his Highgate tenancy provided that he moved to 52 Langbourne Mansions, a smaller apartment just a few doors along; it also wrote off the £1,000 of back rent still owing on the previous flat. Auspiciously enough, the first day of his new tenancy was marked by a television programme about sex changes. He watched it with interest and copied down a sentence from one of the reviews: 'The gratifying feature was that the presentation was severely clinical and the psychological problems of these unfortunate people were not discussed.'

But not all his creditors had given up the chase. 'It is only four weeks ago that I started a job as a general clerk for the princely sum of £12. 10s a week, until I am able to resume my normal vocation as author-lecturer,' he wrote to the electricity board in January 1967, pleading for more time to pay his debts. The job was almost certainly fictitious; in any case, the electricity board started legal proceedings. Unable to afford the £150 fine, he was sent to Pentonville prison for a month.

• • •

After his previous spell in prison, Michael Karoly had advertised himself as an 'odd man' available for dinner parties. Now, on the back page of his Pentonville prison notebook, he drafted the following letter:

Dear Sir,

I saw and liked your advert in the *London Weekly Advertiser*. I have recently moved to London and don't know anybody so I'm taking a chance on replying to you.

I am in my late forties, a widow, lost my only son too at the same time as my husband. To be frank, I have no intention of remarrying nor am I interested in sex for sex's sake, in fact not in any form. What I hope to find is a reasonably presentable and articulate friend as a theatre, cinema, concert, etc. companion – and nothing else – on an expenses shared basis.

For your further information, I am rather tall (5ft 11), wear glasses and use a hearing aid and cannot by any stretch of the imagination be called beautiful. As against that, I think I am quite well-dressed and well-groomed, i.e. suitable for a man to appear in public with, a couple of years at university (sociology and economics) to my credit, having stopped just short of graduating.

If under these conditions you are interested, I am awaiting your reply.

Unencumbered by family, Michael could now write

his own script. As the letter shows, he was already preparing for his most daring feat of method-acting even before his release from Pentonville in February 1967. The letter also suggests that he was self-conscious about his unfeminine appearance and size, so much so that he exaggerated his disabilities: he did not wear glasses or a hearing-aid. In other writings at this time he described his female persona as a horse-faced battle-axe.

Conscious of his humiliation in Hertfordshire – where his disguise had been 'read', to use the transvestite jargon – the big, burly Michael Karoly knew that he couldn't become Charlotte Bach without careful planning and long practice. He looked up obscure articles on cross-dressing, wrote to drag performers such as Danny La Rue and Ricky Renee, and placed an advert in the *New Statesman*:

TRANSVESTISM. Psychologist has professional interest in the subject. Any information or intelligent views will be appreciated and treated in confidence.

About a dozen people replied, including a rubber fetishist and a masochistic clergyman. Another, a transvestite taxi-driver, introduced Michael to a Cuban exile named Ramon who might better be described as a silk fetishist: he didn't like dressing in female clothes because he considered it disrespectful to women, and preferred draping himself in soft, shiny and silky fabrics. The feeling of the material against his skin lifted him on to a 'spiritual plane' where he could experience orgasms lasting six hours – or so he claimed.

Though Ramon met Michael only a few times, he had an enduring influence on the trainee transvestite. Ramon foresaw a future paradise where the feminine principle would reign supreme and coarse, vulgar masculinity would no longer be required: by then women would have found a way of reproducing without men. He also drew Michael's attention to the recurrence of andro-gyny and sexual camouflage in classical literature. It was Ramon who persuaded Michael that he could be a 'spiritual transvestite', for whom the wearing of skirts and tights would be merely the emblem of a mystical quest for feminine archetypes. On 1 May 1967 Michael began work on his book *Man and/or Woman: A Comprehensive Study of the 'Tammuz Complex' (Transvestism)* – Tammuz being the Babylonian god who was castrated by his mother as a fertility offering. Parallels were drawn with similar legends in other cultures in order to prove that modern cross-dressers were the heirs to a timeless and universal tradition.

Not all the text was taken up with such lofty themes, however. Some respondents to his *New Statesman* ad had become friends, for whom he would act as a gentleman escort when they wished to go out as 'femmes', and the book was liberally seasoned with tales of their adventures in which Michael appeared under the pseudonym 'Gregory'.

Gregory is an expansive and likeable self-educated poly-histor. Due to height and facial factors, it is always Gregory who takes Moira [a.k.a. John] out. Let him carry on:

'She usually comes to my place. I have a larger flat and she's got a car. She comes in her best togs, then goes and raids my wardrobe and jewellery box for a fur coat or mink scarf and necklaces and what have you. I've got a lot more stuff: I kept all my wife's things. By the time we go out she's a really presentable old girl. We've been to some of the best places in town, Quaglino's, Hilton Roof, Caprice, you name it. Never any trouble. We always come back to my place for a coffee and a chat, then in the small hours I give her a cuddle, kiss her goodnight and tell her to go home. I haven't a spare room; besides, I wouldn't want to stare into John's ugly puss after such a lovely evening.

'I like taking her out. I couldn't afford to go to those places, so she pays. She enjoys it and I do my best to give her a good time. Quite often in the restaurant, over the brandy, we hold hands. It's sort of in character with an ageing romantic couple. It always makes the waiters go all sentimental. A few times I even got an erection looking at her.'

The importance of transsexuality, according to Charlotte Bach, is 'that it completely disproves the modern psychologist's notions of hetero and homosexuality'. While never going so far as to claim that the desire to mutate into the opposite sex was universal, she did believe that there was 'a sort of unconscious, involuntary drift towards the opposite sex and a more or less unconscious, involuntary resistance to this drift, and the clash between these two currents produces tensions which result in impasses that can only be resolved by means of a creative act, and that all creative acts of any kind are essentially evolutionary moves. Sometimes forward, sometimes backward, but always a change from the existing evolutionary state of the species.' She greatly admired a passage from William Golding's novel *Free Fall* in which the narrator asks a woman: 'What is it like to be you?... What is it like in the bath and lavatory and walking the pavement with shorter steps and high heels? What is it like to know your body breathes this faint perfume which makes my heart burst and my senses swim?' What modern science failed to notice, Charlotte argued, 'is that this seemingly romantic and unimportant fantasising is the root of the entire evolutionary process'.

The motivation of transvestites may be inscrutable to many, but no one can deny the effort and bravery involved. It is one thing to dress yourself to your own satisfaction in front of a mirror, quite another to step outside your own front door and perform humdrum activities – shopping, travelling on a bus, queueing for the cinema – without being embarrassed by the looks and glances you elicit. When you succeed, however, the rewards are intense. Michael's tranvestite friend Deryck/Della Aleksander said that walking down the street in full regalia was like a continuous orgasm.

Aleksander, a London schoolteacher, was a complete novice at cross-dressing when he answered the advertisement in the *New Statesman*. After a couple of meetings, he asked the 'psychologist' why he had such an obsession with transvestism; by way of reply, Michael produced a photo of himself sitting on a sofa with a woman. Aleksander looked once and looked again. Then the penny dropped: both figures were Michael.

Despite Michael's doubts and hesitations, by the summer of 1967 'Charlotte' was showing herself in public, starting with tentative trips to the cinema. Each moment of acceptance – when an usherette addressed her as 'madam', when a bus conductor called her 'dear' – was marked down as a triumph. After a month as Charlotte he would hide away in his flat until his beard regrew, and then emerge as Michael for the following month before reaching for the razor again. It was increasingly hard to maintain the pretence that he had no more than a 'professional interest', especially when he was invited to Oxford by a woman who had seen the advert and wished to introduce him to one of her friends, a transvestite professor.

Just before his visit [she recalled] Michael wrote and said he had become Charlotte, and did I mind if she came rather than Michael? I wrote back to her as Charlotte and said I would be delighted and would meet her at Oxford station. I had no difficulty recognising her because she stood out from the other passengers coming through the barrier. I winced. She was the epitome of all that Oxford in those days disliked in women. Overdressed. Lots of jewellery. 'Bells on her fingers and rings on her toes,' I thought automatically, and looked down at Charlotte's feet which were immaculately clad in a most beautiful pair of thin leather high-heeled shoes. She had red finger nails, false, very long, and black eyelashes and lots of make-up. She looked old...

We had lots of arguments about real femininity. She said that she wanted to be a flighty, foolish woman, the silly-little-me type, as that was the very opposite of what she had been brought up to be – the competent man. I felt that the essence of being a woman lay not in clothes or dependence, but in being compassionate, caring and putting up with pain and discomfort... It was then that she produced her Mother Goddess theory. She said that when she was dressed in her beautiful silk nightwear she could reach an orgasm which had a mystical quality, and this was the sort of sexuality she enjoyed when being a woman. The ecstasy was connected with a kind of celebration of her mother and a rejection of her father.

Eventually the Oxford woman left Charlotte and the professor (who introduced himself as Agnes) to enjoy a 'girls' talk' without the hindrance of a real woman.

Paradoxically, it was at about this time that Michael took a female lover, Audrey, whom he met at a pub in Hampstead. She claims to h ve known at once that he was her kind of man when she saw the book under his arm, *Love and Orgasm*. Their sexual relations continued sporadically until Michael became Charlotte permanently, and Audrey found him 'perfectly normal in bed – fully masculine, even a little male chauvinist'. How can one square this with his professed ambition to be a fluffy, frilly, silly-little-me? A few years later, reminiscing about her early female apprenticeship, Charlotte told Audrey that 'on the one or two occasions when there was something like a sex play with men, I must admit I enjoyed it, but only as long as the person did not know about my past. On the one occasion when I gave in to someone, the moment I realised that his interest centred on the fact that I was not quite a normal woman – indeed the fact that he thought I was a kinky man – I suddenly felt a monster and he seemed like a repulsive insect.' Conveniently enough, Charlotte's subsequent writings include a lengthy explanation of why 'a masculine male courting a feminine transvestite is not really a homosexual' – another example of his tendency to seek out universal theories which would cover his own predilections.

Meanwhile, Michael was still trying to create some kind of social life for himself as a man. He advertised in the *Hampstead & Highgate Express*: 'Informal conversazione group would welcome a few new members, no fees, no committee, no nothing, just friendly intelligent gab.' The discussion group, which met on Sunday afternoons, lasted for a mere three weeks. On the first two occasions there was one other man as well as a woman, Helen Forsyth; by the third Sunday it was down to Michael and Mrs Forsyth. They agreed to call it a day. Before she left, however, Michael told her that he had a confession to make: he once had a twin sister called Charlotte, who was now dead, and whom he loved so much that he felt a compulsion to become her. 'Most men want to love a woman,' he said. 'I want to be a woman. I am a freak!' He then burst into tears. Mrs Forsyth decided that he was going mad, and recommended him to see a doctor at once.

Michael Karoly once wrote an article about the inner sense of self that is essential for 'the new woman'. He quoted a transvestite called Pat, who may or may not have been Michael himself:

I used to have difficulties when getting on to a bus or when I had to negotiate a high kerb. So I bought a flared and pleated skirt which gave me greater freedom of movement. And I used to get odd looks. I can't be sure if anyone actually read me, but it was enough to make me study women even harder and practise at home with the kitchen steps. Yet the looks still kept coming.

Then one day it struck me. If I couldn't move freely in a tight skirt, the trouble was not with the clothes but with me.

Perhaps the secret was not to buy clothes in which I felt comfortable, but to move in such a way that I felt comfortable in normally tight clothes. Practically from the moment I realised this, I found myself getting about much more confidently with no more odd looks.

But the real revelation came some time after this. It happened one day when I was walking down the stairs to the Underground. A woman coming up had a good look at me from my shoes to my hat. She too was tall, well-dressed and about the same age as myself. She was a gee-gee [transvestite argot for a 'genetic girl'], but she was not reading me, I could see that. The look she gave me was a kind of jealous admiration from one woman to another... Before, I was only a visitor; now I felt at home in my clothes.

Michael's comment on this was that 'faith and sense of truth' mattered more than the external props (something he had learned at the Stanislavsky Studio), and Charlotte was now happy to heed the advice of her previous persona, practising self-hypnosis techniques to achieve a 'triumph of the will'. She and Deryck/Della Aleksander also obtained supplies of the female hormone diethyl stilbestrol from a sympathetic doctor at the Charing Cross Hospital. 'We both noted changes,' Aleksander reported, 'not so much in our breast tissue, for that was to be expected, and in any event was only moderate and ceased when ingestion ceased, but markedly in our temperaments; in our mental attitudes, even in the way we approached problems. Our intuitive and emotional lives seemed mysteriously heightened.' Charlotte came to believe that living as a woman boosted her hormones far more than any tablets. On an excursion to a wine bar in Camden, Aleksander (who was playing the male part that evening) listened to two working-class women at the next table while Charlotte went to powder her nose. 'You've been read!' he hissed when her ladyship returned. 'Nonsense,' she retorted, sure that self-confidence would outweigh her physical disadvantages. Drawing herself up to her full height, she went over to the table and asked the two women to join her for a drink. They were then treated to the tear-jerking story of how her 'husband' had died.

'Do you think you'll marry again?' one of the women asked.

'I don't know,' Charlotte sobbed. 'Maybe.'

'He'd have to be a giant!' the other muttered.

In her quest for 'understanding friends of either sex', Charlotte now placed an advertisement in the underground newspaper *International Times*. 'I am in my late forties,' she wrote, 'a graduate of humanities (Ph.D) and

I have the appearance of a tall, well-groomed, well-preserved middle-aged gentlewoman.' The decision to award herself a Ph.D is suggestive – as is the appearance of 'Baroness Charlotte Hajdu' in the British Museum reading room records, in January 1968. There are slips in her name for seven dates in January and February, requesting books on Mithra, lesbianism, gnosticism and Manicheans.

By March, however, Charlotte was Michael once more, beard and all. 'I have sent Charlotte on one of her lengthy holidays,' he wrote, 'so that I can again settle down to do some work. You see, in view of the subject I am working on, I could not achieve the necessary calm detachment with the dear creature hovering around my shoulders.' His particular study at the time was the ten-spiked stickleback, about which Dr Desmond Morris had written a famous academic paper in the 1950s. Michael was so interested that he copied out Morris's work in longhand at the British Museum, then went home and typed it all out again.

Charlotte often spoke about the pivotal role played by the humble stickleback in her 'discoveries', and her summary of Morris's findings explains why:

In spring, their mating season, the sticklebacks move to their regular breeding grounds… In the year when there is enough room, but only just, the tribe will have increased still further. The next year there isn't enough room for all the males to stake out nesting territories. Only the tougher ones will be able to do so; the weaker ones will have to go without. Moreover, since by then they too will have adopted the jet-black nuptial colouring, they will be constantly harassed by the nest-owners since there is no room within the area of suitable breeding grounds which is not the nesting territory of someone.

The harassed and intimidated males begin to lose their black nuptial colouring. Soon they will have readopted their off-season colour which is indistinguishable from the normal female colouring. Some will even develop a swollen belly. If the intimidated male, who now looks like a female, is invited by the nest-owner male dancing the courting dance, he follows. He pauses for a half-minute or so, like an ordinary female. The nest-owner then follows and presumably fertilises the non-existent eggs. The next year the population will have dropped back to normal.

The point that struck Michael was that the male fish, as a pseudo-female, pauses for exactly the same half-minute as the normal female – and thus, as far as one can tell, does not merely go through the motions of being a female but experiences them as well. He took this as proof that all males carry within them a template of female behaviour. Hitherto, while not doubting the authenticity of his female feelings, he had feared that he could never achieve more than a painted pastiche of womanhood. Thanks to Desmond Morris, he now felt sure that 'inversion' – whether in sticklebacks or north London psychologists – was entirely natural and therefore true. What had begun as a safety valve, a way of restoring his masculinity, was now an expression of his femininity – the route to a new version of normality.

. . .

In July 1968, after reading Michael's book *Hypnosis*, Geoff Wood decided to seek help from the author for his own problems. Michael proposed a course of hynotherapy, and asked if a fee of three guineas per session would be all right. This was about a quarter of Wood's weekly wage but after some hesitation he agreed, and for the next six years he was a regular visitor to the flat. Pretty soon attempts at therapy stopped: he was happy just listening to Michael talk.

Despite this fillip to his income, Michael still needed more. He wrote to his transvestite friend John/Moira:

Dear Moira,

I apologise for writing to you like this, but I am in the last stage of desperation. You very kindly agreed to help with Charlotte's hairdo, for which I am very grateful as it is time for her to arrive and I am getting extremely edgy about it. In fact, in the last couple of weeks I could hardly concentrate on my work. Believe me, the compulsion is just as great as any you have experienced. Except that I prefer longer uninterrupted periods instead of the odd evening when one cannot properly get into the role.

Anyway, as it happens, the wig cannot be repaired so I have no alternative but to get another one. Unfortunately this presents quite insurmountable problems to me in my present state of finances. On the other hand, if I put off Charlotte's visit, I gain nothing because I could not carry on working anyway, so the loss would be even greater...

So, as you see, I am in a very desperate state and I am afraid I might do something I would regret afterwards. I wonder if I could impose on you again to the tune of 20 guineas for the wig and two guineas for styling. You will not regret it if you help me once more, but you might be sorry if you find that I have done something desperate.

Similar messages – half-begging, half-threatening – were sent to other friends. A letter to Agnes, the cross-dressing Oxford professor, shows just how unpleasant Charlotte could be towards her benefactors:

Dear Agnes,

Thank you for the photos back. I told you to keep one and you seem to have kept a dozen. While I am greatly flattered by the fact – and your remarks – at the moment I am certainly not in a position to replace them at 2/6d each. Nor, may I put it you, am I Mme La Contessa or Mme La Marquise. You know my name and title, so kindly use that or don't use anything at all.

I note your remarks on the hard times you are going through at the moment. I would be very sorry for you if I believed that you had not budgeted for unforeseen events. But I am sure you have, and you have also assured me that you have budgeted for that *petit cadeau* I am so badly in need of... I have to pay the electricity, gas and telephone now. Furthermore, assuming that you are the sort of person who keeps a promise, I have bought on credit a set of Carmen hair-rollers, which I need now that my hair is getting long enough. Anyway, what about other things I am running out of like nail-varnish remover (Revlon 8/9d a bottle), Lash-on Mascara (Gala 12/6d), tinted foundation (Max Factor Translucent Peach Blossom 12/9d), nail varnish (Revlon Crystalline Cherry Mousse 8/6d) and who knows what else.

And don't say that they are not essential for feeling feminine. They are.

Thank you for your assurance that you would read my book with sympathy if I felt in need of submitting it to you. What you don't seem to realise is that the part you have read is of no great importance. The part I am writing now is what matters. I am disproving Freud thoroughly and offering a much more comprehensive theory of sexuality than he did, much more accurate and, unlike his, mine is supported by scientific evidence which is verifiable by incontrovertible neurophysiological experiments.

In case you don't realise it, Freud was the only person – until my book comes out – who endeavoured to give a scientific theory of sexuality... I am filling in all the areas which are overlooked in all current thinking on sex. It is going to do for psychology what Einstein's theory did for physics, i.e. it will render present-day psychiatry as obsolete as alchemy.

I don't suppose you believe it, but that is of no relevance. You might well see me being offered a Ph.D (Oxon) which I shall refuse unless it is offered through a women's college – and then I shall make a speech in which I mention a certain Magdalen don who let me down in my hour of need. You may smile at my hopes, but you will not smile when I walk into Magdalen in my new mink coat and Yves St Laurent gown and am received by the Provost as the woman who disproved Freud.

From hair-rollers and mascara to Freud and Einstein: the boastfulness, no less than the bullying, was scarcely calculated to endear her to the recipient. When Agnes next came to London, Charlotte suggested that a regular allowance might be in order, and the hints of black-mail became more explicit. It marked the end of their friendship.

Someone must have paid up, however. Over the coming weeks and months, Geoff Wood observed the tall, upright, bearded Michael Karoly alter into a clean-shaven, slightly slouched figure. After the disappearance of the beard, his hair became longer and longer until he started to tie it back, first in a pigtail, then in a bun. When Wood went to the bathroom he began to find hairnets, curlers and make-up – and nylons hanging up to dry. Michael explained that these belonged to a woman friend who sometimes stayed in the flat. Then he took to wearing white cotton gloves, claiming that he had a rash on his hands; when they were taken off, however, Wood noticed that the fingernails were filed to a point, with tiny remnants of nail varnish still visible.

It was only a month after Geoff Wood's first visit that

the 'psychologist' made what was to be his final change from Michael to Charlotte. But for the sake of Wood's company – and three guineas a week – he kept up the pretence of being a man for a further five years.

His identities were becoming increasingly confused. In a letter to Michael White, an old drinking companion from Mayfair, Michael Karoly said that he and his sister were writing a book, which they intended to publish under the pseudonyms 'Mr Michael B. Bach and Miss Charlotte M. Bach'. ('At first we thought of publishing under my name alone, but eventually she will want the credit due to her.') Karoly invited White to the Highgate flat, but it was Charlotte who opened the door. Although surprised, White soon grew accustomed to the new persona, which still seemed rather provisional: when Charlotte lunched with him at his club, where women were not admitted, Michael came instead.

Apart from these occasional quick-change acts, by the summer of 1969 Charlotte had been living as a woman for a year. Every week, however, she would have to become Michael again in order to sign on at the local employment exchange and claim her benefits. Annoyed by this insult to her femininity, she eventually informed social security that she was now a woman. The officials asked for a letter from a doctor or psychiatrist confirming the new identity – to which Charlotte replied testily that no such letter would be necessary since she was neither ill nor mad. This left the staff at the labour exchange in a quandary: they could hardly send her for a job as a woman, but if they found her work as a man she'd undoubtedly turn up in female dress anyway. As long as Charlotte refused to cooperate she was safe from having to take paid employment at all – thus achieving a lifetime's ambition. After two years of fruitless negotiation, officialdom threw in the towel and classified Charlotte M. Bach as unemployable. Henceforth she had to sign on only four times a year.

To celebrate the transition, Charlotte sent Audrey a black-edged card announcing that her brother, Michael Karoly, had died. Audrey felt something like genuine grief: she had accepted Charlotte, but it was Michael who had been so good in bed.

Chapter Five

'Goddess of my dreams'

Roza Hajdu, now living in Venezuela, hadn't heard from her wayward son Carl since his bankruptcy in 1957: despite efforts to trace him through the Red Cross and Hungarian organisations in Britain, he had remained – in her words – 'as silent as a deaf pig'. But in the summer of 1969 Imre Hoefle, a friend from Caracas who was visiting London on business, discovered the existence of 'Michael Karoly' and rang the number in the phone directory. He then made the astonishing discovery that Michael had been superseded by Charlotte.

On his return, Hoefle broke the news to Carl's sister Vilma but couldn't think what to tell the 82-year-old Roza. Guessing that something was being kept from her, Roza pestered Vilma until all was revealed. Surprisingly quickly, she came to accept that she had lost a son but gained a daughter. Charlotte celebrated the renewal of contact with her family by writing to ask for a hand-out.

Many acquaintances of Carl or Michael had always thought him a bit odd, which may have made his final reinvention less of a shock. Even so, it is a tribute to his remarkable powers of persuasion that almost everyone accepted the public emergence of Charlotte without fuss or disgust. Michael Ryan, the Irish caretaker at Langbourne Mansions, said that both Michael and Charlotte were 'model tenants – no trouble at all'. An upstairs neighbour, Marjorie Woolnough, assumed at first that the tall lady at number 52 must be Michael's sister. When Charlotte put her right, Miss Woolnough had only one question: 'Are you happy?' ('Do you know,' Charlotte said, 'you're the first person to ask me that.') The local council transferred the tenancy to Charlotte without demur, and on April Fools' Day 1970 she changed her name by deed poll from Carl Michael Blaise Augustine Hajdu to Charlotte Maria Beatrix Augusta Hajdu. Except in dealings with officials, however, she never used her real surname. It was as Charlotte M. Bach (Ph.D) that she submitted a few chapters of *Homo Mutans, Homo Luminens* – the first of several books she wrote under this title – to London publishers in the spring of 1970; none showed the slightest interest. And it was in the guise of 'Daphne Lyell-Manson' that, later the same year, she began yet another career – as a spanking madam.

Masochism had been second only to transvestism on Michael Karoly's score-card of popular deviations in *Hypnosis*. 'It would be tragicomical beyond belief,' Charlotte had written in 1969, when applying to the Social Science Research Council for funds, 'if I were compelled to do a stint at prostitution, which is the only way to leave myself enough time to do my writing.' In a letter to the Department of Social Security, she had added, 'It is a very lucrative trade and I know I would make a very good living at it (what with my experience both as a man and as a psychologist).'

In December 1970 she placed her first advertisement in *Lonely*, a cheaply printed contact magazine sold in sex-shops: 'Tall, educated, sophisticated, attractive widow. Strong personality, wishes to meet compatible gentleman. Occasional domestic help also wanted.' Readers of *Lonely* understood the code, and over the next six months more than 200 of them – including an African prince, a Harley Street doctor and a retired major in Yorkshire – wrote to Mrs Lyell-Manson. Most received a standard reply asking them to send £2 (as an earnest of goodwill) and a lengthy account of their sexual fantasies. Those who passed muster were then invited to meet Daphne, bringing 'acceptable gifts' such as cigarettes and rosé wine. A man called Brian wrote after his second visit:

> Thank you for seeing me recently. I enjoyed seeing you again and hope this feeling was reciprocated. You looked captivating when I arrived, and even more so later when wearing dark stockings and black slip. After the way you dealt with me, I regard you with a good deal more respect than previously, and even a little fear. It hurt me more than I had anticipated and was a lesson to me to be punctual and more courteous in greeting you. I realise that you will probably be more severe in future and, indeed, will need to be if you are to impress upon me your complete authority. It was considerate of you to minister to me afterwards. I much appreciate your kindness, and felt much in need of it too! Severity, then tenderness – wonderful.

The inveterate actor Karoly Hajdu was no less convincing as a dominatrix than he had been as a baron or a hypnotherapist. Here is a testimonial from another sore but satisfied customer:

As you instructed me, Madam, I lay in my bed on my return and relived the events of the evening. I had myself in the most painful and erotic situations with you always so coolly in command, an absolute autocrat, intent on being completely and utterly obeyed. I kissed your feet as a token of my subjection to your authority and carefully, slowly, plied kisses inch by inch creeping higher and higher up your lovely ivory legs. I reached the silken smoothness at the top of your thighs. I hardly dared lift my eyes to see the treasure that lay but an inch from my face, for I had thoughts of you madam without your pretty panties and soft shadowy curves I knew would disappear beneath the tantalising curls to meet again as your darling soft sweet pussy, but before I dare pay homage at the very temple of love, I am challenged. With terrible authority you take me to task for taking such an outrageous liberty and, taking your cruel long cane, chastise me sharply on my naked buttocks.

And another:

Goddess of my dreams… It was lovely to fondle your legs and feet. From the tone of your letter I had expected you to be very severe and was surprised how loveable and gentle you are. You were most generous and kind to spend so much energy on my ugly male backside. You drink considerable quantities of rosé wine. It seems a shame that all that alcohol should run to waste when you have finished it. No doubt if you secured me so that I could not resist, you could, by physical persuasion, induce in me a craving for a brew so delightfully created.

Yet another humble servant confessed to wondering what it would be like to have a woman bugger him with a dildo. For her part, Mrs Lyell-Manson used the proceeds to buy herself a new cooker.

The adverts and correspondence petered out in the summer of 1971 – not least because Charlotte's mother arrived in London for a visit. (Roza Hajdu, now 84, had spent four weeks in Hungary, where she passed round photographs of her new-found daughter with touching maternal pride.) But Daphne's adventures in the spanking trade bore fruit a couple of years later in Charlotte's modestly titled manuscript 'On the Basic Axioms or Lemmata of a Universal Theory of Relativity', where she argued that deviations such as sadomasochism provide a 'vivid theatre' in which otherwise obscure processes and characteristics can be viewed more clearly.

Charlotte's own sexual theatrics were now confined to discreet performances in the back row of the stalls with a man she had met at a local cinema. Though she never knew his name, they fell into a routine of dining every Wednesday evening at a nearby Wimpy Bar before going to a movie. During the adverts and trailers, as she told a friend, she would play with his 'thing' while he fondled her thigh. 'He ejaculated, heaved a sigh, went off to the loo to clean himself up and returned looking very pleased with life.' They then watched the main feature, after which Charlotte caught the bus home. She sometimes wondered why she kept up this anonymous dalliance with a man 'whose intellect does not even come up to my ankle', and whose conversation consist-ed almost entirely of 'What film shall we see tonight?' or 'Did you get your bus all right last week?' Her answer was that shamans should have some sort of sex life to reinforce their 'emergent creativity'. Thus the joyless ritual continued for several years – until, in the spring of 1979, she bought a colour television and never went to the cinema again. One of her acolytes noticed that 'some of the life seemed to go out of her; imperceptibly, something seemed not quite the same as before'.

• • •

All his life, Michael Karoly had lived in the shadow of his female persona – sometimes glimpsed tantalisingly in a mirror, at other times lodged in Harrods' depository. When Charlotte first entered his life he still insisted that masculine Michael Karoly could write more objectively about inversion than this flighty creature, who sought only to distract him from serious work with her excited chatter about make-up and hairstyles. Later, when Charlotte was stepping out more confidently, she found the actual experience of being a woman strikingly different from what she had imagined – especially when feminine men came to worship at the feet of this matronly 'absolute autocrat'. Having explored the wilder shores of sex and returned with her sense of self robustly intact, she had nothing left to fear from submerged desires.

As a consummate performer, however, she was still frustrated by the lack of an audience. Adverts in the *New Statesman* and elsewhere ('Intelligent conversazione on sex and human behaviour, Saturday evenings, Hampstead') brought a few inquisitive young men into her orbit, some of whom were so dazzled by the intellectual authority of this lonely widow that they became fully fledged acolytes. The most devoted was Don Smith, a sadomasochistic drop-out who had decided that the answers to life's larger questions were more likely to be found in the gutter than in a university library. 'She told me that of all the people who attended her talks I was the one who instinctively understood her theory best,' he said, 'and the one who was closest to being a shaman in the tradition of the ancient shamans.' Although Smith had no idea what this meant, he was suitably flattered, and during the 1970s produced several pamphlets summarising her ideas, each of which sold between 500 and 1,000 copies.

Charlotte's belief that sexual deviation was the mainspring of evolution also made her a popular speaker at gay meetings. The secretary of the London Monday Group for Homosexual Equality, which met every week at a pub in Bayswater, recalled 'a lovely evening when the late Dr Charlotte Bach frightened us so much we did not dare get up for a pee, never mind a drink.'

When Charlotte addressed the lesbian group Sappho, Don Smith was banished to the bar downstairs as 'anatomical males' weren't allowed in; none of the sapphists thought to question the political correctness of Charlotte's own anatomy. Nor did Smith. 'I did wonder for perhaps the first half of the first lecture I attended,' he admitted after her death, 'but what she was telling us seemed to be so wholly fresh and new that I could hardly think such a wise person could be perpetrating a deception over something as basic as her sex.

In gay liberation circles we joked about what might be the size of her clitoris, especially after Charlotte had spoken about the Dahomey women massaging their clitorises to make them resemble penises, but I really feel we all took Charlotte as a woman – a masculine one, but then we were feminine men anyway.'

Cult status was not enough to satisfy her rapidly swelling ambitions. Academics, television executives and journalists began to receive lengthy samples from her work-in-progress, accompanied by letters suggesting that anyone who publicised her ideas on sexuality – 'which are going to render almost all of current psychology and psychiatry as obsolete as alchemy' – could bask in reflected glory when she won her inevitable Nobel Prize. Polite incomprehension was the usual reaction. Graham Massey, editor of the BBC documentary series *Horizon*, thanked Charlotte for the typescript but confessed that 'I do not see how it would fit into the programme that we are currently engaged on… It may well be that someone else is interested in your work.'

Hardly anyone was. The press baron Lord Thomson declined Charlotte's generous offer to act as a consultant to the science editors of the *Times* and the *Sunday Times*, despite her claim to have 'formulated a radically new theory of non-dimensional space-time continuum'.

She wrote to the Archbishop of Canterbury announcing that there is no supernatural agency in the universe, and that God is a human invention. 'I do not think that the Archbishop will agree without cavil,' an assistant at Lambeth Palace replied. A letter to John Waddington Ltd reveals just how obscure and eclectic her researches had become – and how desperate was her yearning for fame and wealth:

> I understand your firm is the leading manufacturer of playing cards and games and that you are always on the look-out for novelties in this field.
>
> Enclosed herewith please find reproductions of two pages from an ancient Aztec codex; kindly take a look at them.
>
> I am a philosopher-psychologist, former lecturer at the University of Budapest. For the past few years I have been engaged in some rather abstruse socio-anthropological research. In the course of this work, as a sort of 'spin-off', I happen to have cracked the code of the Aztec-Maya-Omec Tonalpouhalli ('ritual year'). This, even if I say so myself, is quite an important academic achievement and will undoubtedly create quite a stir in the appropriate circles when I publish my findings.
>
> For your information – in case your acquaintance with the extinct Meso-American cultures is no longer up to specialist

standard – the Tonalpouhalli was a 'year' consisting of 13 20-day 'months'... The Nahuatl word 'Tonalpouhalli' translates as something like 'the arithmetic of destiny' and it forms the foundation of the Tonalamatl ('The Book of Fate') which consists of pictures only...

The reason I am telling you this is that, with the riddle solved, the Tonalamatl lends itself eminently well to a transformation into a game akin to the phenomenally successful Monopoly, as well as to an ordinary card game, as well as to a divinatory system similar to the Tarot cards... I feel that this holds considerable commercial possibilities.

Messrs Waddington felt otherwise.

Not all Charlotte's appeals fell on stony ground. As we have seen, the author Colin Wilson became an enthusiastic cheerleader. Brian Lewis, the professor of educational technology at the Open University, used some of his research budget to run off 100 copies of Charlotte's manuscript, which she then sold at her weekly talks. She also struck up a correspondence with Grey Walter, one of the earliest researchers into patterns of electrical activity in the human brain. As always happened if a male academic showed any interest in her work, she sent him photos of herself and added flirtatious postscripts. When he eventually suggested that they meet, she proposed dinner at the Post House in Hampstead – 'and afterwards we can, perhaps, come back to my place for a cup of coffee. Perhaps, provided you don't start behaving like an amorous goat. Anyway, I am big enough and strong enough to take care of myself; if you don't behave, I shall spank you like a schoolkid.' Walter protested that at 65 he was far too old for such frolics, and proved the point when they returned to Langbourne Mansions after a heavy dinner in Hampstead: while Charlotte Bach started giving him the benefit of her infinite wisdom, Grey Walter fell fast asleep.

Brian Goodwin, a lecturer in biology at Sussex University, was curious enough to invite Charlotte Bach (Ph.D) down to Brighton to speak to his students. Irked by their manifest incomprehension, she concluded by declaring huffily that she would shortly be awarded a Nobel Prize. 'It was not the usual kind of seminar, as you can imagine,' Goodwin said. 'The material she presented was difficult to assimilate, ranged very widely, and it was the force of her personality that came over most clearly.'

This was the common reaction to Charlotte's public performances: even if what she actually said was as incomprehensible as a Russian opera, there was no doubting her status as a prima donna. Word of this extraordinary creature soon spread through the academic bush telegraph. In May 1973 she participated in a one-day conference – titled 'Beyond Materialism' – at the Institute of Education in London; a fellow-speaker, Dr Ralph Yarrow, then asked her to give a talk on 'Maleness and Femaleness in the 20th Century' at Keele University; someone in the 200-strong audience at Keele recommended her in turn to Dr Daniel Davidson, who was arranging a series of lectures on 'Creativity' at the Exeter College of Art. As Davidson recalls:

She had a riveting presence which, whether you were sympathetic or not, you couldn't ignore. As it was, she had no immediate feedback from our stunned faces, although she didn't seem to mind and may even have enjoyed 'blowing our minds' into paralysis. I had the feeling that she enjoyed demonstrating the capacity of the human mind to function at full pitch in much the same way that a great singer might love to demonstrate the capacity of the human voice.

Visually she was striking. Someone described her as being like a tank with a flower poking out of the gun barrel because she had this huge presence and a tiny delicate rose in her lapel and a chintzy ribbon in her hair.

Nature may not have blessed Charlotte Bach with great beauty, but she made the most of what she had. As Colin Wilson observed, she had 'a positive hunger' for attention. When Wilson chaired a debate on the paranormal between two popular authors, Lyall Watson and John Taylor, at the Royal Institution in the summer of 1976, Charlotte seated herself prominently in the centre of the front row – wearing a huge hat and waving an equally enormous fan.

When the speakers seemed to be drawing too much attention [Wilson wrote], she used the fan vigorously, putting them both off their stride. When question time came, she immediately signalled me with her fan; as a friend, I naturally had to call upon her to speak. She rose magnificently to her feet, and her deep voice echoed through the room; she seemed to be saying, 'Enough of these amateurs, this is how it ought to be done.' It was a superb exhibition of one-upmanship. And because I was chairman, she succeeded in making several more interjections. When I addressed her as 'Doctor Charlotte Bach' she seemed to grow even larger...

While Charlotte was wowing them down at the Royal Institution, another of her followers decided he had had enough. For four years she had been using Bob Bayford's flat in Hampstead for her talks without ever paying the rent originally agreed. He was fed up with her overweening conceit, her expectations of total obedience, her assumption that no intelligent person could have the slightest reservation about the smallest detail of her work. Her frequent mentions of the Nobel Prize were more than he could bear.

Fortunately for Charlotte, other disciples such as Don Smith were still willing to humour her. Smith once told her that she seemed to him like a second Jesus; after brooding for some minutes she said no, not Jesus, she was more of a John the Baptist, paving the way for a greater shaman who would be the founder of the next phase of human civilisation. Another admirer, a wealthy doctor called Michael Kirkman, even endowed an institute in her honour, the Kirkman-Bach College of Human Ethology – though the impressive title of this seat of learning was scarcely matched by its address, a small flat in Belsize Park Gardens. A programme of lectures at the 'college', advertised in *Time Out* in July 1975, gives the flavour of Charlotte's exotic and eclectic syllabus:

1.) Symbology of fetish in homosexual/sadomasochistic rituals (with slides).

2.) Anatomy of the battered baby syndrome.

3.) Causative factors in homosexual promiscuity (with slides).

4.) Symbol-logic in Chinese ideogrammatic writing.

5.) Concepts of quantum-jump and cybernetic feedback loop in the Yang-Shao culture of China, 2500BC (with slides).

These lectures are specially recommended to psychotherapists, psychiatric social workers, cyberneticians, biophysicists and students of allied disciplines. Human ethology, the revolutionary evolutionary theory, is the intelligent way to creative self-liberation. Open house discussions every Thursday, 8pm (£1).

Charlotte asked Desmond Morris to become a patron of the college, but her breathtaking tactlessness guaranteed a refusal. The invitation read more like a blackmailer's ultimatum:

Cooperate with me and you are opening the door for yourself for a Nobel Prize of your own, or ignore my offer and condemn yourself to remain for the rest of your life a third-rate academic in a third-rate college who may have made his packet in popular publishing but is despised so much more for it by smug, bone-headed academics. And the real irony of it is that you haven't really got much of a choice in the matter. Others have a choice to be my friends or my enemies. You haven't… If not more than one tenth of my conclusions are found to be valid, you will be seen to have held the key of a scientific goldmine in your hand and thrown it away. And that will make you not only a third-rate academic in a third-rate college, but a first-rate fool not only in the eyes of fellow academics but, being a well-known popular writer, in the eyes of the whole world.

Desmond Morris was puzzled, as well he might be. 'I am intrigued to know what kind of response in me you expect to provoke by being so offensively condescending,' he replied. 'Are you deliberately trying to drum up opposition? I do think this is a pity. I also think that it is a pity that you have chosen to misapply the word "ethology" to your work. Why can't you present your ideas simply, in clear scientific language, without all this shrill table-thumping?' Unabashed, Charlotte continued to badger Morris for many months; she appeared genuinely unable to believe that he would pass up an opportunity to become even more famous. 'You may wonder why I am bothering to write this letter to you,' she told him in 1980. 'Well, I was 60 years old almost to the day when I wrote my previous letter… That my work will be fully vindicated in the long run is beyond the slightest shadow of a doubt. The point is I want to be still around in full possession of my faculties when it happens. That's all.'

Weary of wasting her genius on the desert air, Charlotte was at last feeling her age. 'As far as my book is concerned, everything is proceeding, although very slowly,' she wrote gloomily to her mother. 'I am still waiting for full recognition from the world scientific community.' One small consolation was the news that a publishing house had commissioned Charlotte's friend Dr Mike Roth to write a book about her work; but then the publisher went bust.

• • •

After her 60th birthday on 9 February 1980, the Department of Social Security started paying Dr Bach a widow's pension until it realised the mistake and put her back on social security. She complained to Don Smith of a 'heaviness in the bowels' – brought on, she suspected, by eating too many grapes. By Easter 1981 her ankles were badly swollen. She told Don Smith that she had 'the shits' again, blaming it on the fact that her water heater had been out of action for several weeks: Charlotte, ever a stickler for cleanliness, was now obliged to take her morning baths in cold water. She seldom left the flat, and the favoured few who were allowed to visit often found her muttering about food poisoning. Yet the post-mortem report prepared after her death in June described her as 'a well-nourished man'.

Even after the posthumous discovery of the truth about her gender, most friends continued to refer to Charlotte as 'she' – not only from force of habit but because it seemed disrespectful to reimpose on her the maleness which she had taken such extraordinary pains to escape. 'Why do you think I am so careful about myself?' she wrote to Della Aleksander in 1970, in the early stages of her transformation. 'I know that I can't get away with it forever, but I want to make the grade before anyone gets wise.'

The dreams of fame and Nobel prizes may have been absurd, but by carrying her secret almost to the grave she did 'make the grade'. Transvestism is not simply a matter of changing one's wardrobe: every aspect of behaviour has to be re-learnt, and a new sense of self created. The task was all the harder for Charlotte, with her deep voice and mannish physique. Yet she carried it off with style, conviction and courage. It would be ungenerous, after witnessing such heroism, to say that she was 'really a man'. Which man? In her final identity she achieved an authenticity that gave her far more pleasure and fulfilment than any of the feckless personae she inhabited previously. Mightn't one reasonably conclude that it was her life as a man that had been the masquerade – that Baron Hajdu and Michael Karoly were the great pretenders, whereas Dr Charlotte Bach was not only her finest creation but also her true self?

Francis Wheen is the bestselling author of Karl Marx (Fourth Estate, 1999) and How Mumbo-Jumbo Conquered the World (Fourth Estate, 2004). He is deputy editor of Private Eye, and a former Guardian columnist. He lives in Essex, and has two young sons.

Other titles published by SHORT BOOKS:

**I'm A Teacher
Get Me Out of Here!
by Francis Gilbert**

At last, here it is. The book that tells you the unvarnished
truth about teaching. By turns hilarious, sobering, and
downright horrifying, I'm a Teacher, Get me Out of Here
contains the sort of information that you won't find in any
school prospecti, government adverts, newspaper articles, or Hollywood film. In this astonishing memoir,
Francis Gilbert candidly describes the remarkable way in
which he was trained to be a teacher, his terrifying first
lesson and his even more frightening experiences in his
first job at Truss comprehensive, one of the worst
schools in the country. Follow Gilbert on his rollercoaster
journey through the world that is the English education
system; encounter thuggish and charming children, terrible and brilliant teachers; learn about the sinister effects
of school inspectors and the teacher's disease of 'con-
troloholism'. Spy on what really goes on behind the
closed doors of inner-city schools.

———

1-904095-68-2

**My Brief Career
The trials of a young lawyer
by Harry Mount**

My Brief Career, Harry Mount's hilarious account of his hellish year as a "pupil" – a trainee barrister in The Temple – has all the horror of a Dickensian tragedy and all the charm of Bridget Jones' Diaries. An exposé of what goes on behind the ancient walls of London's inns of court, this fascinating story dares to reveal the grim secrets of one of England's most archaic institutions...This is a book for everyone who has ever thought they might want to become a lawyer.

———

1-904095-69-0

GOING BUDDHIST
Panic and emptiness, the Buddha and me
by Peter J Conradi

'Sweating, shaking, pain, giddiness, hyperventilation,
guts locked in painful spasm...
A claustrophobic terror of being abandoned in a
desolate place...'

It often takes a crisis to see what a life's shape has
been, to show what really matters. For Peter Conradi,
writer, academic, acclaimed biographer of Iris Murdoch,
the moment came in 1982.

This is his account of the new life-journey he embarked
on back then. It is a self-help book for cynics, totally
unpatronising, full of wise comedy, in which it quickly
becomes clear that "going Buddhist" is neither a quick
fix, nor a one-shot deal. Over many years, Conradi and
his friend and mentor Iris Murdoch discussed the meaning of religion, its place in the world, and the Buddhist
pursuit of 'Good'. Drawing on their letters and conversations, he seeks to explain the point of a religion now
more relevant than ever to Westerners, perishing from
the knowingness and nihilism of the age.

1-904095-63-1